Causal Inferences in
Nonexperimental Research

Causal Inferences in
Nonexperimental Research

by

HUBERT M. BLALOCK, JR.

The Norton Library

W · W · NORTON & COMPANY · INC ·
NEW YORK

Books That Live
The Norton imprint on a book means that in the publisher's
estimation it is a book not for a single season but for the years.
W. W. Norton & Company, Inc.

Library of Congress Cataloging in Publication Data

Blalock, Hubert M.
  Causal inferences in nonexperimental research.

  Includes bibliographies.
  1. Social sciences—Mathematical models.   I.   Title.
[H61.B48   1972]   300'.1'51   72-2903
ISBN 0-393-00642-5

To my parents and Jimmy

Preface

   This short book represents an effort to pull together materials on causal inferences that are widely scattered in the philosophical, statistical, and social science literatures. There are, of course, a vast number of writings on the subject of causality, and no brief attempt to summarize these works could hope to succeed. My aim has been much less ambitious. It has been to sort out those ideas which seem to be most useful to the practicing social scientist who must, somehow or another, make sense out of his data. Causal interpretations will undoubtedly be extremely useful if not necessary for a long time to come. If so, it is advisable to attempt to spell out the rules of causal inference, even where the underlying logic is only imperfectly understood.

   Many of the ideas and concepts that appear in this work can undoubtedly be expressed more satisfactorily in mathematical or logical terms. However, it seems preferable at this stage to present these ideas in ordinary language that can be understood by social scientists who are not technically trained. While a knowledge of applied statistics through multiple regression analysis is assumed, no more than simple algebra is required. Nevertheless, it is anticipated that readers will vary considerably with respect to mathematical and statistical backgrounds. Those with relatively little training in these fields are apt to experience difficulty with Chapters II and V, as well as the initial sections of Chapter III. Therefore in order to improve readability I have included a summary chapter which lists the major arguments of each chapter point-by-point (with page references). Some readers may find it helpful to read the summary of each chapter before attempting to follow the detailed arguments.

Perhaps an autobiographical note will be useful in order to give the reader an idea of why this book was written. As a social scientist originally trained in mathematics and physics, I found myself floundering in the field of methodology in which there seemed to be well-understood principles of inference in some areas and no valid guides in others. As a graduate student I was told such things as, "Sociology *can* be a science," and "One must always control for relevant variables." I was also exposed to the usual controversies regarding operationalism, functionalism, and the reality of groups. But discussions of these topics never seemed satisfactory.

I also noted, with frustration, that whereas the statistician had specified definite rules of inference for probability samples drawn from fixed populations, many of these rules did not seem to cover adequately the kinds of situations with which the social scientist often deals. In particular, there seemed to be a point beyond which the statistician's rules did not go and where actual practice seemed to involve *ad hoc* types of inference. Later, I learned that some of the reasons for this gap are owing to the shortcomings of social science research—involving substantial measurement errors, the inability to randomize and replicate, a high percentage of unexplained variation, and numerous unmeasured variables and unclear concepts. Nevertheless, such shortcomings will be with us for a long time to come, and it therefore seemed advisable to attempt to formulate some preliminary rules of inference which allow for these complications. I hope that other persons with more technical training will be able to provide solutions of a more definitive nature.

Needless to say, I did not find the field uncharted. The more I studied the subject, the more I realized that econometricians, in particular, have made considerable headway. But I also assume, erroneously perhaps, that most social scientists in other fields are generally unaware of the technical work being done on such problems as the use of structural equations, identification, multicollinearity, measurement errors, and the like. I have therefore tried to integrate some of this work into my own discussion, though in a completely nontechnical manner. As will be readily apparent, I owe a special intellectual debt to Herbert Simon and Herman Wold, whose ideas on causal models are fundamental to the presentation in Chapters II and III. I strongly urge the technically trained reader to examine the works of these authors and the general econometrics literature much more thoroughly than will be possible in the present work. Even though the techniques may not be appropriate for the cruder data of the other social sciences, the approaches used may nevertheless be highly suggestive.

I would like to thank the Ford Foundation for a grant extended through its program for assisting American university presses in the publication of works in the humanities and the social sciences, and the Social Science Research Council and Yale University for providing released time for this study. My appreciation, also, to Richard F. Curtis, O. Dudley Duncan, Elton F. Jackson, Gerhard E. Lenski, and Daniel O. Price for reading and criticizing portions of the earlier manuscript. Betty Galloway, Alys Venable, Randall Lord, and the staff of the University of North Carolina Press have also provided considerable help with typing, computations and editorial assistance. Permission to reproduce material in Chapter III that appeared in *Social Forces* and in the *American Anthropologist* has been granted by the editors of these journals.

Finally, my thanks to my wife, Ann, and to our children for their patience and fortitude.

Table of Contents

Tables

Causal Inferences in
Nonexperimental Research

I

Introduction

The logic of experimental designs is reasonably well understood. By careful manipulations the experimenter can isolate the separate effects of several independent variables operating simultaneously on a single dependent variable. Through devices such as randomization he can also rule out on probability grounds certain possible disturbing influences that are unmeasured or unknown. Even randomization, of course, cannot take care of some types of variables that may inadvertently be introduced through the experimenter's manipulations. But a well-designed experiment enables the scientist to get by with a relatively small number of simplifying assumptions that are reasonably plausible. If he then wishes to make causal inferences on the basis of his results he can do so with some degree of confidence, though causality can never be proved beyond all doubt no matter what the nature of one's empirical evidence.

The situation becomes much more complex whenever the scientist must deal with observational data, though in principle the same rules of inference can be applied. This is especially true whenever one is studying a system that is not effectively isolated, so that large numbers of outside influences are likely to be operating. Not only is it difficult to rule out many of these variables through randomization, but the observer also lacks adequate information about the temporal sequences involved. This is particularly likely in the case of comparative research where one's information is confined to a single point in time. In such instances the problem is by no means as hopeless as is implied in the simple assertion that correlation does not prove causality. Whenever certain crucial pieces of information are not given, however, it becomes necessary to make additional simplifying assumptions that may be much less plausible than in the case of the more or less ideal experiment.

The primary purpose of this short book is to explore the problem of making causal inferences on the basis of data from nonexperimental studies. The emphasis is on the word *explore*, since no attempt at a highly formal treatment will be made. The discussion will be addressed mainly to the practicing social scientist, rather than the mathematician or philosopher of science.

After laying the foundation in the remainder of this chapter and in Chapter II, I will deal with specific causal models and the nature of the assumptions that must be made in order to make causal inferences on the basis of correlational data. Many of the models are extremely simple and require unrealistic assumptions. But, if we are to judge by historical developments in the natural sciences, it is best to begin with relatively simple models and assumptions that can then be gradually modified and made more complex.

The discussion may therefore be primarily of heuristic rather than immediate practical value to sociologists and other social scientists whose measurement techniques, control over extraneous variables, and theoretical tools may not yet be adequate to the task of making causal inferences. Nevertheless, I am convinced that issues similar to those discussed in the present work must at some point be faced in all of the nonexperimental social sciences. Significantly, the greatest progress in this area seems to have been made by the econometricians, whose subject-matter field is most advanced in terms of being susceptible to careful quantitative treatment.

The best justification for attempting to deal with this difficult problem, perhaps somewhat prematurely, is that in actual research we find social scientists attempting to make causal inferences even where the underlying rationale is not at all clear. For example, a common practice is to introduce control variables through statistical manipulations of one sort or another. Suppose one controls for education or sex and finds a reduction in the original correlation between X and Y. Even where temporal sequences are known, can he therefore infer a spurious relationship? Exactly what must be assumed in order to infer spuriousness? Should one also examine the behavior of slopes as well as correlation coefficients? Under what causal conditions can we expect slopes to remain unchanged with the introduction of controls even where correlations are altered?

The fact that causal inferences are made with considerable risk of error does not, of course, mean that they should not be made at all. For it is difficult to imagine the development and testing of social science theory without such inferences. Since they are in fact being made in practical research, it is necessary to understand more clearly the nature of the scientific rules that underlie their use.

CAUSAL THINKING, THEORY, AND OPERATIONALISM

The problem of causality is part of the much larger question of the nature of the scientific method and, in particular, the problem of the relationship between theory and research. *There appears to be an inherent gap between the languages of theory and research* which can never be bridged in a completely satisfactory way. One *thinks* in terms of a theoretical language that contains notions such as causes, forces, systems, and properties. But one's *tests* are made in terms of covariations, operations, and pointer readings. Although a concept such as "mass" may be conceived theoretically or metaphysically as a property, it is only a pious opinion, in Eddington's words, that "mass" as a property is equivalent to "mass" as inferred from pointer readings.[1]

The extreme empiricist or operationalist attack on theory has been made and answered. There is no need to review this controversy except to mention that many of the objections to causal thinking involve the same types of issues. We shall take the commonly accepted position that science contains two distinct languages or ways of defining concepts, which will be referred to simply as the theoretical and operational languages. There appears to be no purely logical way of bridging the gap between these languages. Concepts in the one language are associated with those in the other merely by convention or agreement among scientists.[2]

The empiricist criticism of certain types of theoretical thinking contained valid arguments, but it went too far. It has made us aware, however, that it is by no means a simple matter to develop theories that are directly or even indirectly testable. Causal thinking has also come under the attack of logical positivists, operationalists, and other types of empiricist philosophers. According to Mario Bunge, "The causal principle fell into disrepute during the first half of our century as an effect of two independently acting causes: the criticisms of empiricist philosophers, and the growing use in science and technology of statistical ideas and methods."[3]

One admits that causal thinking belongs completely on the theoretical level and that causal laws can never be demonstrated empirically. But this does not mean that it is not helpful to *think* causally and to develop causal models that have implications that are indirectly testable. In working with these models it will be necessary to make use of a whole series of untestable simplifying assumptions, so that even when a given model

1. Arthur S. Eddington, *The Nature of the Physical World* (New York: The Macmillan Company, 1933), pp. 251-55.

2. For an excellent discussion of this question, see F. S. C. Northrop, *The Logic of the Sciences and the Humanities* (New York: The Macmillan Company, 1947), Chapters 3-7.

3. Mario Bunge, "Causality, Chance, and Law," *American Scientist*, XLIX (December, 1961), 432.

yields correct empirical predictions, this does not mean that its correctness can be demonstrated.

Reality, or at least our perception of reality, admittedly consists of ongoing processes. No two events are ever exactly repeated, nor does any object or organism remain precisely the same from one moment to the next.[4] And yet, if we are ever to understand the nature of the real world, we must act and think as though events are repeated and as if objects do have properties that remain constant for some period of time, however short. Unless we permit ourselves to make such simple types of assumptions, we shall never be able to generalize beyond the single and unique event.

At the same time, we recognize that certain of these assumptions will be more realistic than others. Some objects may for all practical purposes be assumed to have constant properties over long periods of time; but the properties of others may change almost as rapidly as we measure them, or in fact may change precisely because we do measure them. Some events are so similar to others that it is no strain on one's imagination to think in terms of repetitions (or replications) of the "same" event. In other instances, while there may be a certain amount of regularity, there is also a high degree of what might appear to be random variation superimposed on whatever regular patterns may be found.

One way of dealing with the problem is to make use of theoretical models of reality. In developing these models the scientist temporarily forgets about the real world. Instead, he may think in terms of discrete "somethings," or systems, made up of other kinds of somethings (subsystems, elements) which have fixed properties and which act, or can be made to act, in predictable ways.

John D. Trimmer points out that a very common mode of thought consists of conceiving of models in which systems are acted upon and respond in certain ways.[5] The process can be

4. This particular point is emphasized in Karl Pearson's classic, *The Grammar of Science* (1957 ed.; New York: The Meridian Library, 1957), Chapter 5.

5. John D. Trimmer, *Response of Physical Systems* (New York: John Wiley & Sons, 1950), pp. 1-3.

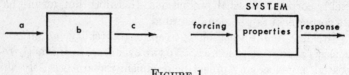

FIGURE 1

diagrammed as in Figure 1. There are of course a number of different terms which can be used to stand for *a*, *b*, and *c*, and Trimmer arbitrarily selects the concepts "forcings," "properties," and "responses." Unlike its real-world counterpart, the theoretical model can also contain a clear-cut distinction between the system and everything outside the system, or its environment. Forcings can then be unambiguously attributed to the environment, and responses can be assumed to be caused by the joint operation of external forcings and system properties. Systems can also be decomposed analytically into elements, which themselves can be conceived as systems in their own right. The scientist can then readily pass back and forth between macro- and micro-levels of analysis.

In the imaginary world of the theorist, events can be repeated and properties may be taken as constant. By using such abstract models, the scientist can then make certain predictions about what should occur under given conditions. He then returns to the world of reality and attempts to assess how well his predictions work. If they work, the model is retained; if not, it is modified in favor of one that gives more accurate predictions.

The dilemma of the scientist is to select models that are at the same time simple enough to permit him to think with the aid of the model but also sufficiently realistic that the simplifications required do not lead to predictions that are highly inaccurate. The more complex the model, the more difficult it becomes to decide exactly which modifications to make and which new variables to introduce. Put simply, the basic dilemma faced in all sciences is that of how much to oversimplify reality.

THE CONCEPT OF CAUSALITY

The concepts of forcings and causes are obviously closely related, as are the notions of responses and effects. In fact, they might be considered identical in meaning. I shall not attempt to give formal definitions of any of these terms, and it indeed may turn out wise to treat the notion of causality as primitive or undefined, as Francis suggests.[6]

According to Bunge, one of the essential ingredients in the scientist's conception of a cause is the idea of "producing," a notion that seems basically similar to that of forcing.[7] *If X is a cause of Y, we have in mind that a change in X produces a change in Y and not merely that a change in X is followed by or associated with a change in Y.* Thus although the idea of constant conjunction may be made a part of one's definition of causality, conjunction is not sufficient to distinguish a causal relationship from other types of associations. For example, day is always followed by night, and childhood by adolescence, but we do not think of the first phenomenon in each pair as a cause of the second. The idea of production or forcing is absent; days do not produce nights.

Bunge argues that this notion of a cause as a producing agent makes it difficult to translate the concept into abstract logical or mathematical languages.[8] Producing refers to an ontological process, i.e., to what exists in the real world. It is something over and above what can be expressed in formal languages. Likewise, it has a reality apart from the observer and his perceptions. We can, of course, study epistemologically how the scientist finds out about the real world and the limitations of the perceptive and descriptive processes. But causal principles are quite distinct from man's abilities to describe or formulate these principles, and—according to Bunge—we must not mix the two.[9] For example, it would be misleading to

6. Roy G. Francis, *The Rhetoric of Science* (Minneapolis: The University of Minnesota Press, 1961), p. 127.

7. Mario Bunge, *Causality* (Cambridge: Harvard University Press, 1959), pp. 46-48.

8. *Ibid.*, pp. 239-45.

9. *Ibid.*, pp. 326-27.

confuse causal notions with those of prediction, the latter referring to the state of man's knowledge about the real world.

The obvious empiricist objection to the idea that causes involve a producing or forcing phenomenon is that we cannot possibly observe or measure such forcings. Perhaps the best we can do is to note covariations together with temporal sequences. But the mere fact that X and Y vary together in a predictable way, and that a change in X always precedes the change in Y, can never assure us that X has produced a change in Y. We can, however, predict certain empirical relationships between the two variables. As we shall see in the next chapter, the notion of prediction is often used, particularly in the statistical literature, in order to get around this empiricist objection to causal terminology. But this substitution of prediction for causal statements involves some of the same kinds of difficulties as does extreme operationalism, as we shall subsequently note. Among other things, it does not permit one to think theoretically, and often it does not allow adequately for asymmetrical relationships.

The inclusion of the notion of production or forcings introduces asymmetry into the relationship between cause and effect, though we may also handle instances of what might be termed "reciprocal causation." If X causes Y, then a change in X produces a change in Y, but it does not follow that a change in Y produces a change in X. Thus a change in rainfall produces a change in wheat yields, but a change in wheat yields does not necessarily produce a change in rainfall. The fact that temporal sequences are also asymmetrical helps empirically to resolve the direction of influence question; the rainfall occurs first, and then the wheat grows. But since the forcing or producing idea is not contained in the notion of temporal sequences, as just noted, our conception of causality should not depend on temporal sequences, except for the impossibility of an effect preceding its cause.[10]

10. *Ibid.*, pp. 62-71 See also Herbert A. Simon, *Models of Man* (New York: John Wiley & Sons, 1957), pp. 12-13.

The concept of cause may be used in a narrow sense of a forcing coming from outside of the system under study. Presumably, an outside force acts upon the system and produces a response of some kind. But the system has certain properties which indeed may be quite complex, and these properties also influence the response in some way. One may choose to refer to these properties as "conditions" rather than as causal agents in their own right. Bunge, for example, confines the notion of cause to outside agents, since he wishes to distinguish causal laws from other types of deterministic laws.[11] But we shall not restrict our usage to externally produced events. It must be remembered that one's choice of a system's boundaries is always to some extent arbitrary. What for one person is a forcing from the environment, for another may involve an internal change.

Having discussed in a general sort of way the ideas we wish to convey with the notion of causality, let us postpone further discussion of the more exact manner in which we shall use the term in our attempts to develop and make inferences about causal models. Discussion of reciprocal causation and the problem of prediction will also be postponed. We turn next to a brief consideration of certain objections to causal thinking.

SOME PROBLEMS WITH CAUSAL THINKING

The literature on the subject of causality is of course vast and cannot be summarized in any simple manner. We shall confine ourselves primarily to certain kinds of objections that focus on the problem of the gap between theory and research and our ability to verify causal laws empirically.[12] Let us begin

11. Bunge, *Causality*, pp. 17-19.

12. Other kinds of objections can also be raised. For example, one may point to the unfortunate tendency for social scientists to use one-to-one causal thinking, in the sense that each effect is assumed to have only one cause. Such thinking can of course lead to serious jurisdictional disputes; witness the debates over various single-factor causal theories.

with an example furnished by Philipp Frank, who, as we shall see, argues that causal laws are essentially working assumptions or tools of the scientist rather than verifiable statements about reality.[13]

Frank asks us to imagine two iron bars resting on a table. This is state A of the system. Left to themselves the rods will not move, and therefore state A is followed by another state A that is indistinguishable from the first. But now suppose we replace one of the bars by another bar, identical with the original bar except for the fact that it has been magnetized. The bars will now move toward each other, i.e., state A is followed by state B rather than A. Suppose someone were unaware that one of the bars had been magnetized. He might conclude that the original states in the two situations were identical "in all relevant respects." But if so, the laws of causality would apparently be violated. To quote Frank: "In order to be able to say that the law of causality is still valid, we must say that the initial states were only apparently the same. We must include in 'state' not only the totality of perceptible properties, but also another, namely, in our example, magnetization."[14] *One can thus always introduce new postulated properties or variables in such a way that causal laws cannot possibly be negated.*

Causal laws, then, are assumed by the scientist. When they appear to be violated, he reformulates them so as to account for existing facts. For example, in noting that two bars move together in an apparently inexplicable way, one may postulate the existence of some previously unsuspected property (e.g., magnetism). In such a manner he may discover new variables and formulate revised causal laws that predict to a wider range of empirical phenomena. But he cannot directly assess the validity of the causal principle itself. It becomes merely a highly useful theoretical tool.[15]

13. Philipp Frank, *Modern Science and its Philosophy* (New York: Collier Books, 1961), Chapter 1.

14. *Ibid.*, p. 65.

15. *Ibid.*, pp. 65-66.

Bertrand Russell notes that causal laws are really only applicable to a completely isolated system.[16]   We cannot prove that a system is isolated.   Instead, we only infer this from the fact that uniformities or causal laws hold for the system in question.   If the laws were completely known in advance, the isolation of a system could be deduced from them.   For example, laws of gravitation could be used to infer the practical isolation of the solar system.   Isolated systems have no special importance in the finished structure of science.   But they can be very useful in enabling the scientist to discover these laws.[17]

Frank emphasizes that the principle of causality cannot be refuted if we are permitted to postulate or introduce new variables.   Russell points out that a system must be isolated—that is, free from outside forcings—if causal laws are to be appropriate.   *Clearly, a causal relationship between two variables cannot be evaluated empirically unless we can make certain simplifying assumptions about other variables* (e.g., no environmental forcings or postulated properties operating in unknown ways).   Causal statements or laws are purely hypothetical, as Bunge indicates.[18]   They are of the *if-then* form.   *If* a system is isolated or *if* there are no other variables operating, *then* a change in A produces a change in B.

It is because of this hypothetical nature of causal laws that they can never be tested empirically, in the strictest sense of the word.   Since it will always be possible that some unknown forces may be operating to disturb a given causal relationship, or to lead us to believe a causal relationship exists when in fact it does not, the only way we can make causal inferences at all is to make simplifying assumptions about such disturbing influences.

At one time it may have been thought that we might proceed otherwise.   John Stuart Mill proposed a set of canons for causal inferences based on experimental observations: the famous

16. Bertrand Russell, *Mysticism and Logic and Other Essays* (New York: W. W. Norton & Company, 1929), p. 198.

17. *Ibid.*, pp. 198-99.

18. Bunge, *Causality*, pp. 35-36.

methods of agreement, difference, and concomitant variations.[19] A careful examination of Mill's proposals, however, turns up certain phrases such as "alike in all relevant variables but one" or "having only one circumstance in common," which expose the real inadequacies of the methods. As Cohen and Nagel point out, Mill's proposed methods cannot be used as methods either of discovery of relevant variables or of proof of causation.[20] At best, they can be used only to enable one to eliminate inadequate causal arguments. The basic difficulty is a fundamental one: there seems to be no systematic way of knowing for sure whether or not one has located all of the relevant variables. Nor do we have any foolproof procedures for deciding which variables to use.

CAUSAL MODELS

Herbert Simon prefers to confine the notion of causality to hypothetical "models ' that are not subject to many of the limitations and criticisms that would apply to discussions of the real world.[21] For example, we can always imagine an idealized model in which events are exactly repeated, whereas in reality we can agree with Karl Pearson that no two events are ever exactly the same.[22] Such models permit us to think in terms of perfect replications and to bypass Pearson's argument that it is only because of the crudity of our conceptual and measurement apparatus that we tend to think of event A as always being followed by event B.[23] Similarly, by thinking in terms of models we need not be concerned with our inability to demonstrate causality in the real world.

In view of the general nature of the problems encountered when we attempt to bridge the gap between theory and research, Simon's proposal seems quite sensible. However, it will prob-

19. An excellent discussion of Mill's methods can be found in Morris R. Cohen and Ernest Nagel, *An Introduction to Logic and Scientific Method* (New York: Harcourt, Brace, Inc., 1934), Chapter 13.

20. *Ibid.*, Chapter 13.

21. Simon, *Models of Man*, pp. 10-12.

22. See Pearson, *The Grammar of Science*, pp. 152-56.

23. *Ibid.*, pp. 156-59.

ably be extremely difficult for most persons, including the present writer, to get along without the aid of a metaphysical assumption to the effect that something akin to causal laws operates in the real world and not just in the hypothetical models of the scientist. But such an assumption amounts only to a "pious opinion" and cannot be demonstrated by any methods presently known.

Following Simon, we shall conceptualize causality in terms of simplified models. We must start with a finite number of specified variables. Obviously, a good deal of thought and research would be necessary prior to the decision as to exactly which variables to include in the system. But once having made this decision, we must confine ourselves to these explicit variables, though we may introduce error terms to take care of the effects of whatever variables we have not considered. If the model proves inadequate, then we may wish to introduce additional variables or modify the model in other ways, but at least for the time being we must confine our attention to a specific set of variables. Otherwise, we cannot derive testable conclusions from the model. Having thus committed ourselves to this particular choice of variables, we in effect admit that had another set been selected, our model might have looked quite different. In other words, there is nothing absolute about any particular model, nor is it true that if two models make use of different variables, either one or the other must in some sense be "wrong."

The Determinism Issue. Having selected a specific set of variables, we may make the model either completely deterministic or probabilistic. In the former instance we argue that if X causes Y, then if we were to hold constant all other causes of Y (as assumed in the model under consideration), and if we were to manipulate the value of X, the value of Y should also vary in a completely prescribed way so as to trace out a perfect mathematical function of some sort. There should be no errors involved, and it would be possible to predict the value of Y perfectly if we knew X. Had different numerical values of the control variables been selected, we might conceivably have obtained somewhat different mathematical functions, though in any given instance we conceive of these other variables as being completely controlled.

But in order to make the causal model more realistic or in keeping with its real-world counterpart where systems are not completely isolated, we shall introduce error terms into the equations. Even where we assume that all other known causes of Y have been controlled, we allow for variation in Y which is not caused by variables explicitly included in the system. The perfect mathematical function involving exact predictability is replaced by the regression equation in which we trace the *mean* Y value for each value of X.

The introduction of such error terms is consistent with either a deterministic or indeterministic metaphysical position. We may either imagine the variations in Y to be owing to outside variables that have not been brought into the causal model, or we may think of their being owing to "chance" or random processes. While we shall make use of the first formulation, which is deterministic, it will not make any difference in practice which position we take. Since in real-life situations it will be impossible to take account of all relevant variables, or to obtain perfect measurements, we shall never be in a position to resolve the determinism-indeterminism controversy by empirical means.

The deterministic position has this advantage, however. Whenever we find a high degree of unexplained variation, we immediately look for other variables that have not been included in the causal system, expecting that we can successively reduce this variation by adding further variables. But in terms of any given model, one can take his choice as to metaphysical assumptions, and there need be no controversy over the determinism issue.

Allowances for unknown causal variables that produce changes in the dependent variable thus make it possible to reconcile causal determinism with statistical laws. But why not attempt to state such laws in nonstatistical terms? Nagel points out that one reason why "laws" in the social sciences are statistical in nature is that they are stated as though applicable to real-world situations rather than ideal ones.[24] Truly universal laws, holding without exception, can never be expected to apply to real situations because of the influence of disturbing factors. Nagel argues that the law of falling bodies, for example, would have to be stated in statistical terms if we were to expect it to apply to empirical situations of all sorts. Instead, it is formulated universally, but the conditions under which it is assumed to hold are both explicitly stated and highly restrictive. For instance, it is appropriate only in a perfect vacuum, which is of course never found in the real world.

We are reminded of Max Weber's discussion of ideal types.[25] Why not formulate our causal laws and other theories in terms of these ideal models and completely isolated systems, then noting how the real world deviates from such a model? In one sense, this is the strategy we shall advocate in the case of causal models. But there is a practical question as to how far we can go in this matter, and the answer seems to depend, in part, on the degree to which experimentation is possible. It must be remembered that the physicist can often approximate the ideal situation to a relatively high degree. Furthermore, he can sometimes even measure the deviation from the ideal and extrapolate his results. For example, we can imagine experiments in which closer and closer approximations to a perfect vacuum are attained. Presumably, one's empirical results should then get more and more similar to the predicted ones under these conditions. Likewise, the physicist can measure the time of descent of a ball on an inclined plane, using surfaces with differing degrees of smoothness.[26]

When experimentation is not feasible, or where even in experimental situations we cannot begin to control for numerous disturbing influences, the situation is quite different. How could we ever evaluate the accuracy of a causal law stated in

24. Ernest Nagel, *The Structure of Science* (New York: Harcourt, Brace, and World, Inc., 1961), pp. 505-9.

25. For a discussion of Weber's ideal types, see Talcott Parsons, *The Structure of Social Action* (Glencoe: The Free Press, 1949), pp. 601-10.

26. Astronomers of course do not usually experiment, but they most often deal with relatively isolated systems that are close approximations to the ideal.

universalistic terminology appropriate to ideal situations? We can admit that such universal laws are theoretically preferable to statistical formulations. But unless ideal conditions can be closely approximated, or until social scientists are in a position to enumerate and measure most of the important disturbing influences, it would seem preferable to state causal laws in statistical terms so that we can explicitly allow for unexplained variation. Such statistical formulations, however, must involve definite assumptions about *how* the uncontrolled variables are operating.

Direct and Indirect Causes. It should be emphasized that the notions of "direct" and "indirect" causes will always be relative to the particular variables included in the theoretical system. For example, suppose we take per cent Negro as a direct cause of discrimination. One can always object that the relationship is "really" indirect and mediated by the intervening variable "prejudice." Assuming that we are referring to the macroscopic level of analysis, one could conceivably obtain indicators of the average prejudice level for a number of communities, in which case he might prefer to take the relationship between per cent Negro and discrimination as indirect. But clearly, it will usually always be possible to insert a very large number of additional variables between any two supposedly directly related factors. We must stop somewhere and consider the theoretical system closed.

Practically, we may choose to stop at the point where the additional variables are either difficult or expensive to measure, or where they have not been associated with any operations at all. In Chapter V we shall consider the possibility of including such unmeasured variables in a causal system. Meanwhile, we shall assume that all variables included have been associated with specific operational procedures. The point we wish to emphasize, however, is that *a relationship that is direct in one theoretical system may be indirect in another*, or it may even be taken as spurious.

As implied earlier, we shall allow for the influence of outside variables by introducing error terms into the analysis. This means that although we can still think of changes in X producing very specific changes in Y, we shall have to look empirically for instances of changes in X linked with changes in *mean* values of Y. In other words, since other factors may affect Y as well, there will be a certain frequency distribution in the changes in Y even where the X's have been always changed by the same amount. We shall have to assume, however, that outside influences have no systematic effects on the relationship between X and Y. To be specific, *we shall assume that the mean change in Y, for a given change in X, is the same as the change that would always occur if all outside influences could be rigidly controlled.*

We are now in a position to give a working definition of what we mean by a direct causal relationship, though we shall not attempt a really formal one. *We first assume that all other variables explicitly included in the causal model have been controlled or do not vary.* Making the additional assumptions about outside variables, we shall then say that X *is a direct cause of Y if and only if a change in X produces a change in the mean value of Y.* The notion of "all relevant variables being held constant" now has a definite meaning, since we are considering a finite and explicitly formulated list of such variables.

There are several difficulties with the above definition, some of which we have already noted. In the first place, we can never tell empirically whether the change in X "produced" the change in Y. All we can observe is a change in X followed by a change in Y. Secondly, one may always object that a certain additional variable should have been included in the causal system, and we shall have to admit this possibility. The inclusion of further variables may alter the causal model almost completely. Finally, we shall later have to introduce an exception to the notion that all of the remaining explicitly considered variables have been held constant. We shall not wish to control for variables which are taken to be causally *dependent* on both X and Y. This may possibly introduce some circularity into our working definition of a direct causal relationship, but we shall leave it to the logicians to resolve the issue.

An indirect causal relationship can then be very simply described. Writing a direct causal relationship between X and Y as $X{\rightarrow}Y$, we shall say that X *is an indirect cause of another variable Z if and only if we can find a subset of variables U, V, ..., W, all of which have been explicitly included in the causal system, such that $X{\rightarrow}U{\rightarrow}V...{\rightarrow}W{\rightarrow}Z$*. The term "intervening variable" will be used to refer to variables such as U, V, and W that stand intermediate in a causal sequence between an "initial" or antecedent cause, such as X, and the final effect Z.

Quite obviously, the notions of antecedent causes and intervening variables are always relative to the particular variables selected in the theoretical system. If we do not admit this fact, we immediately become involved in endless debates over ultimate or original causes, or over the numerous possible causes that have been inevitably left out of our causal system. It is for this reason that we must again emphasize, at the risk of being repetitious, that we prefer to think in terms of causal models that represent highly oversimplified versions of the real world.

Evaluating Causal Models.   Having selected a causal model, we then move in two directions.   We attempt to think by means of the causal model and to make use of our causal assumptions to arrive at certain predictions that can be translated into testable hypotheses.   At the same time, we at least imagine some operational procedures that can be used to test our conclusions. Our ideal in the first instance is some sort of deductive system of reasoning; in the second, it is the perfect experiment.

The most highly developed tool we have available for thinking in terms of causal models is mathematical reasoning.   To anticipate our later arguments, we can make use of a set of simultaneous equations written in such a manner as to allow for the possibility of asymmetrical causal relationships.   These equations, plus certain assumptions about the error terms (e.g., outside variables), permit us to make predictions about the magnitudes of correlation and regression coefficients.   These predictions are then checked against the data.   If they hold within reasonable limits, we retain the model.   If not, we reject or alter it.   But since a number of alternative models also could have yielded correct predictions, we cannot establish any given model as the single correct one. Perhaps we can deduce differential predictions between two competing models, however, in which case we may be able to collect additional data that will enable us to rule out one or the other (or perhaps both) as being inadequate.

In putting the predictions of the model to a test, we also run into very real deviations from the experimental ideal. There will always be measurement error, and we shall have to make certain simplifying assumptions about how these errors are distributed. Some of the variables in the causal system will not be measured at all. Others may not be satisfactorily controlled, owing perhaps to the small size of the sample. And equally as serious, those variables that have been left outside of the causal system may not actually operate as assumed; they may produce effects that are nonrandom and that may become confounded with those of the variables directly under consideration. Through devices such as randomization we can get by with reasonably plausible simplifying assumptions about outside variables. But, as will presently be seen, randomization cannot be used to rule out the disturbing effects of all types of outside variables.

In practice, even the most carefully designed experiment falls short of the ideal. But departures from the ideal are matters of degree, and therefore so is the plausibility of any simplifying assumptions that must be made. Generally speaking, the greater the departure from the ideal experiment and from completely isolated systems, the larger the number of variables that must be explicitly brought into the causal model. And the larger the number of such variables, the simpler our assumptions must be about how they all fit together. We must therefore pay a considerable price whenever we find it impossible to experiment or to study isolated systems. Exactly how much we must pay depends upon a number of factors, some of which will be considered later.

INFERENCES FROM EXPERIMENTAL AND
NONEXPERIMENTAL DESIGNS

The metaphysical assumption that in the real world there
are certain agents that produce changes in the states of a system has its counterpart in the laboratory experiment in which
the investigator actually acts as such an agent. The idea is
that if X is a cause of Y, and if it were possible to hold constant
all other causes of Y, an experimental manipulation of the independent variable X (i.e., an externally produced change in
X) should be accompanied by an observed change in Y. The
change in Y may not occur before the change in X if we are to
infer that Y is causally dependent on X.

The notion of causality implies, then, that if X is changed Y
will also change, provided other causal variables are held constant. But in view of the fact that one never knows in real-life
situations whether or not all other such variables are constant,
we cannot infer that X causes Y merely from our observation
that a manipulation of X is associated with a change in Y. In
other words, while we would be willing to assume that *something*
has produced a change in Y, we cannot be sure that it was our
manipulation of X that did this. We must assume either that
all other causes of Y have literally been held constant or that,
if not held constant, the effects of these variables can safely be
ignored.

Following Kish, we find it useful to distinguish among four
types of variables that are capable of producing changes in Y.[27]
First, there is the particular independent variable (or variables)
with which we are directly concerned and which we are attempting to manipulate. Second, there may be a number of variables
that are potential causes of Y but that do not vary in the experimental situation. Presumably, many of these variables
have been explicitly brought under control and are known to

27. See Leslie Kish, "Some Statistical Problems in Research Design," *American Sociological Review*, XXIV (June, 1959), 328-38. For a more general
discussion of causal inferences from experimental designs, see Claire Selltiz, *et
al., Research Methods in Social Relations* (rev. ed.; New York: Holt, Rinehart
and Winston, 1961), pp. 94-127.

the investigator. There may be still others that are unknown but that just happen not to vary during the course of the experiment and therefore that cannot be used to account for variations in Y. The objective of scientific experimentation is, of course, to bring as many variables as is feasible into this second category.

But there are two other classes of variables that must be considered. Both are either unmeasured or unknown to the investigator, or at the very most, he may be aware of their existence but unable to assess their effects. The third class of variables consists of all variables that are not under control and that do produce changes in Y during the course of the experiment, but that have effects on Y which are unrelated to those of X, the independent variable under consideration.

The fourth type involves variables the effects of which are in some way systematically related to those of the independent variable X, so that the influences of these variables will be confounded with those of X. One possible way for a confounding influence to operate would be for such a variable to be a cause of both X and Y. What appeared to be a direct influence of X on Y might be covariation owing to this third variable. Or in attempting to manipulate X, the experimenter might inadvertently manipulate this third variable as well.

In the ideal experiment there would be no variables of types 3 or 4, and presumably any changes in Y could be ascribed to changes in X. The problem of measurement errors in Y can be conceptualized in terms of variables of types 3 and 4, if we wish.[28] Thus changes in the measured values of Y may be owing not only to actual changes in Y, but may be produced by factors such as the physiological state of the observer. In the perfect experiment, of course, measurement errors are assumed nonexistent.

As Kish points out, the purpose of significance tests is to permit inferences concerning the effects of the independent variable X as compared with those of variables of type 3 which are producing variations in Y that are unrelated to the X scores.[29]

28. The problem of measurement error will be discussed in Chapters II and V.
29. Kish "Statistical Problems," *Am. Soc. Rev.*, p. 331.

It should be noted that such significance tests are appropriate regardless of whether or not type 4 variables are operating, though they cannot be used to rule out disturbing effects of these latter variables.

It is of course through the process of randomization that variables of type 4 are hopefully transformed into type 3 variables, the effects of which are independent of the experimental variable under investigation. As textbooks on experimental design clearly emphasize, the use of control variables, randomization, and significance tests are in no sense to be considered as alternative strategies. Rather, they should (ideally) all be used in experimental designs. First, we control for as many variables as is feasible, given the limitations of the experimental design. Our objective is to turn as many type 3 and 4 variables as possible into type 2 variables. Then we assign individuals to treatments randomly, so as to rule out self-selection. In so doing, we reduce the number of confounding variables. Finally, with the recognition that we will always be left with at least some type 3 variables, we make use of significance tests.

To emphasize that the advantages of randomization in experimental situations are only relative and never absolute, as compared with the results obtained in nonexperimental studies, we must stress the fact that *only certain types of confounding variables can be eliminated through randomization.* Incidentally, we would also argue that the simple rule that significance tests are appropriate only in experimental situations is highly misleading. The mere fact that nonexperimental studies may have a higher proportion of type 4 influences than experimental studies does not mean that one should thereby ignore the effects of type 3 variables in nonexperimental situations.

In order to see the limitations of randomization in eliminating type 4 confounding effects, let us make use of the distinction between forcings and properties. Presumably, we consider responses to be caused by two kinds of causal variables: (1) those that are impinging from the outside environment, and that we have called forcings, and (2) those that we conceive to be properties of the system at the time of observation. Not all properties are thought of as causal forces, of course. But we quite often conceive of internal mechanisms or "driving forces" within the system which combine with the outside forcings to help determine the response. In the case of persons, we think in terms of various sorts of producing mechanisms; witness our inability to get along without notions such as instincts, drives, motives, needs, and goals.

It is quite apparent that when we randomize persons by assigning them to groups according to a table of random numbers, we are only eliminating or reducing the effects of whatever *property* variables might possibly confound our results. There may be certain personality differences that may exist between individuals which might be distributed nonrandomly if self-selection were allowed to operate.

But how do forcing variables enter the picture? We are considering any variables that may operate on the individual from the outside, as it were. We take his present properties as given, though perhaps unknown. The fact that such properties may have in part been determined by past forcings is irrelevant. The effects of the past are presumed "summed up" in present properties. One forcing variable, of course, is the experimental variable itself. The experimenter *does* something to the subjects and then *observes* their responses. But what about other forcing variables that may have slipped in unnoticed by the experimenter? The mere fact that persons have been randomly assigned to groups rules out systematic effects of property variables, but how can such randomization affect forcing variables? Clearly, we randomize people (or other types of units), but not forcings.

The only known way we can bring forcing variables under control is consciously to be aware of their possible existence and to design the experiment so as to take their effects into consideration. In other words, forcing variables of type 4 are turned into variables of type 2, rather than into type 3 variables that are presumed to create only random disturbances. The probability of confounding forcing variables being unnoticed can be reduced by careful design, but at some point the experimenter must stop and make the simplifying assumption that such variables have negligible effects. Otherwise, he cannot make any causal inferences at all.

The point we are emphasizing is that *no matter how elaborate the design, certain simplifying assumptions must always be made. In particular, we must at some point assume that the effects of confounding factors are negligible. Randomization helps to rule out some of such variables, but the plausibility of this particular kind of simplifying assumption is always a question of degree. We wish to underscore this fact in order to stress the underlying similarity between the logic of making causal inferences on the basis of experimental and nonexperimental designs.*

CONCLUDING REMARKS

The purpose of this introductory chapter has been to provide a basis for later chapters in which specific problems of interest to social scientists will be raised. The difficulties that will be later encountered are, for the most part, directly related to many of the problems already discussed. In particular, it will be necessary to make a series of simplifying assumptions, many of which will be inherently untestable. By making these assumptions explicit, we shall in effect be deliberately calling the reader's attention to the difficulties involved in making causal inferences and to the validity of empiricist objections to causal thinking. But at the same time, we hope to demonstrate the utility of causal analysis as a theoretical tool that is useful in the conceptualization of a number of methodological problems.

The reader will find in the concluding chapter a point-by-point summary of Chapters I through V. Before proceeding to Chapter II, it may be helpful for review purposes to read the summary of Chapter I, together with that of Chapter II. It is hoped that such periodic reviews will be particularly useful to those readers who are relatively unfamiliar with mathematical and statistical materials.

II

Mathematical Representations of Causal Models

Mathematics is a theoretical language as contrasted with an operational one. But mathematics is not the same theoretical language as that involving causes and effects. In essence, one uses *three* distinct languages when expressing causal ideas in mathematical terms and evaluating these theoretical ideas empirically: a causal language, a mathematical language, and an operational language.

With three such languages and the necessity of passing back and forth from the one to the other, the likelihood of becoming confused is increased, unless we can establish and understand the meaning of a clear-cut set of rules for making the translations. Unfortunately, the problems encountered are too complex to be treated in more than a cursory fashion in the present work. Yet, without some rudimentary understanding of the issues, we run the risk of considerable fruitless debate and failure in communication.

Perhaps it will be easiest to begin with a simple example from physics. Take the formula $F = Ma$. This is a mathematical equation that expresses the equivalence of a force with mass times acceleration. If we wish, we may even use such a formula to define mathematically what we mean by a force, presuming that one already understands what is meant by the concepts "mass" and "acceleration."

But in the causal language, we may wish to make certain types of metaphysical assumptions to the effect that forces exist in some real sense and that such forces are to be taken as causes or producing agents. Thus we think of a force as something that *produces* a change in the velocity of a body with a given mass. The force, when applied to the body, "causes" it to change its velocity in some unknowable sense. We might take both the notions of force and mass as primitive or undefined in this particular causal language. In referring to the translation in the mathematical language, we might say that a force can be represented by a vector, having both direction and magnitude, but the idea of producing disappears.

We also have an operational language consisting of instructions for measuring at least some of these concepts. Distance may be measured by means of a ruler and time with a stopwatch. Velocity is not measured directly, but is computed (mathematically) as distance/time. Likewise, acceleration is computed as distance/ time/ time or as velocity/ time. Mass is measured by inference in terms of the body's weight at sea level. Here, the operational language involves only a relatively small number of variables that are directly measured by independent means. This "language" is thus very incomplete, but when combined with the mathematical language, it enables one to make a large number of different types of empirical verifications. Certain variables, such as force, may remain undefined operationally and measured only inferentially. If we have already determined a body's mass, and if we can apply the force through a number of replications and note that the acceleration produced is relatively constant from one experiment to the next, we may infer that the force has a particular magnitude.

When a theory is well understood, there will be minimal confusion in passing back and forth from the one language to the other. Thus although the notion of "cause" does not appear in the mathematical expression, this need not bother us. As Bunge points out, relationships such as $F = Ma$ or $PV = k$ (pressure times volume = a constant) merely express relationships among variables that might be conceived as properties or states of a system.[1] If we like, we may rewrite such equations in terms of change relationships, e.g.,

$$\frac{\delta F}{\delta t} = M\frac{\delta a}{\delta t} \qquad \text{and} \qquad -\frac{dP}{P} = \frac{dV}{V}.$$

The first of these equations says that a change of one unit in the force is associated with a change in acceleration of M units. The second equation links a change in volume with a change in pressure.   We can then make the translation that a change in force (or volume) produces a given change in acceleration (or pressure) if we have already agreed that such a translation is legitimate.

The whole matter depends, then, on our ability to specify the rules for going back and forth from one language to another. We shall not be concerned with the very complex issue of translating from the operational language to mathematics.   Suffice it to say that in order for clear-cut interpretations to be possible, the operations in mathematics (e.g., addition and subtraction) must have certain counterparts in physical operations.   For example, one can add two weights by placing them on the same side of a balance.   Operationally, one can place a two-gram weight and a three-gram weight on the same side and obtain a pointer reading of zero when a weight of five grams is placed on the other side.   Likewise, one can add or subtract incomes by physically exchanging dollars.   Or he can subtract three inches from a board by sawing off a portion.   But he cannot subtract I.Q.'s in a similar manner because of the lack of a unit of measurement.[2]

There are a number of decisions that must be made in trans-

1. Mario Bunge, "Causality, Chance, and Law," *American Scientist*, XLIX (December, 1961), 433-34.

2. For excellent discussions of this general problem, see Morris R. Cohen and Ernest Nagel, *An Introduction to Logic and Scientific Method* (New York: Harcourt, Brace, Inc., 1934), Chapter 15; and Clyde H. Coombs, "Theory and Methods of Social Measurement," in L. Festinger and D. Katz (eds.), *Research Methods in the Behavioral Sciences* (New York: Dryden Press, 1953), Chapter 11.

lating between mathematics and a language involving causal terminology. One of the most important problems is that of not permitting too much flexibility in the mathematical system since the paper-and-pencil operations of the mathematician are in one sense much more easy to accomplish than are the physical operations in an experimental setting. Our concern with this type of problem will be postponed, however, until we have dealt with the question of the advisability of confining one's attention to mathematical and logical systems involving attributes and simple classification schemes.

CAUSALITY, ATTRIBUTES, AND NECESSARY CONDITIONS

Causality is often discussed in terms of attributes. For example, it may be said that if A is a cause of B, then B should be present if and only if A is also present. Or we might claim that A causes B if A is both a necessary and sufficient condition for B. The idea of production of course does not appear in the above conceptions, but we can always add the forcing or producing notion to such a definition of a causal relationship. In our subsequent discussion we shall ignore this particular issue and concentrate instead on the question of whether or not it is desirable to restrict one's definition of cause and effect relationships to simple attributes.

One difficulty with the notion that causes involve necessary and sufficient relationships consists in the all or nothing requirement implied. In real-life situations we seldom encounter instances where B is present if and only if A is also present. This would require zero cells in both diagonals of a 2×2 table as follows:

	A present	A absent
B present	100	0
B absent	0	100

We note, of course, that although the notions of necessity and sufficiency imply zero cells, the converse does not hold. The mere fact that we can find no instances in which A is present and B absent, or in which A is absent and B present, does not mean that there is a necessary or sufficient relationship. Since it is always possible that we may later come up with cases in these cells, it follows that we can never demonstrate necessity or sufficiency empirically, although we can show them to be incorrect.

A major problem, in addition, involves the likelihood that there will be more than one condition for B. For example, B may be present not only when A is present but also when C or D are present. Stefan Nowak's excellent discussion of the various possibilities indicates the complexity of the problem.[3] We might take A as a cause of B under any of the following conditions:

1. A is both a necessary and sufficient condition for B
2. A is a necessary but not a sufficient condition for B (i.e., A must be present, but B need not always follow A)
3. A is a sufficient but not a necessary condition for B (i.e., B is always present when A is, but B may also occur when A is not present)
4. A is only partly necessary and/or sufficient for B (i.e., A must *usually* be present for B to occur, etc.).

Strictly speaking, any of the last three situations can be reduced to the first by the device of redefining what is included under "A" or "B." For example, if B must occur whenever A, C, or D occur, we may let A' include the possibilities that A or C or D occur, in which case we may claim that A' is both a necessary and sufficient condition for B. But whereas such redefinitions are technically possible, they are often highly impractical and clumsy. As we have previously indicated, we shall find it advisable to allow for uncontrolled variables, unmeasured factors, and error terms. As Francis points out, even the simple allowance for measurement errors means that we will rarely, if ever, get zero cells.[4] This, in turn, means that it will be difficult to operate with simple categoric logic.

3. Stefan Nowak, "Some Problems of Causal Interpretation of Statistical Relationships," *Philosophy of Science*, XXVII (January, 1960), 23-38.

4. Roy G. Francis, *The Rhetoric of Science* (Minneapolis: The University of Minnesota Press, 1961), pp. 31-32, and 60-61.

But we have a still more fundamental objection to confining our thinking to the notion of necessary and sufficient conditions. Whereas it is admittedly technically possible to think always in terms of attributes and dichotomies, one wonders how practical this is. There are most certainly a number of variables which are best conceived as continuously distributed, even though we may find it difficult to measure them operationally in terms of a specified unit of some kind. We leave it an open question as to the relative proportion of variables that are best conceived as attributes.[5] But if we confine our conception of causality to these attributes, we shall encounter considerable difficulties with continuous variates. On the other hand, we can always take a continuous variable and dichotomize it if we wish. In effect, this means that we can do whatever formal and theoretical thinking we please in terms of continuous variables and then dichotomize these later if we choose to do so.

We therefore elect to discuss causality in terms of continuous variables. We shall treat attributes as a special case by the simple device of restricting ourselves to a "variable" with only two values (e.g., 1 and 0, present or absent). Measures such as percentage differences, ordinarily used to summarize attribute data, can be handled as special cases of slopes.[6] As we shall see, however, certain problems will be encountered with attribute data, in part because of difficulties in selecting nonarbitrary cutpoints. In moving from continuous variates to attributes, we also need to watch out for certain types of assumptions, such as the normality of a frequency distribution. Such problems will not be considered in the present work since they are primarily statistical in nature.

Suppose we have two continuously distributed variables X and Y that are linearly related as in Figure 2. As the scattergram has been drawn, the degree of relationship is nearly perfect. In the limit, we can imagine all points to be exactly on the line

5. Karl Pearson, in *The Grammar of Science* (1957 ed.; New York: The Meridian Library, 1957), Chapter 5, clearly implies that the use of categorized data is but a crude way of handling variables that are often best conceived as continuous variables.

6. This question will be dealt with in somewhat greater detail in Chapter IV.

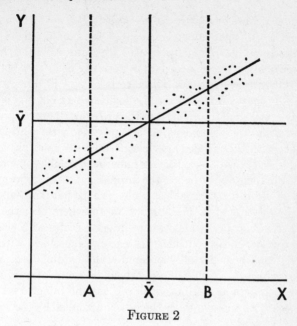

FIGURE 2

if we wish. Now suppose we dichotomize both X and Y into "high" and "low" scores (or alternatively into high scores "present" or "absent"). Clearly, the empirical outcome depends upon our choice of cutpoints. If we cut X and Y in such a way that the intersection of the horizontal and vertical lines falls exactly on the regression line, then we shall obtain results such as those in I below.

But if we cut X at A, keeping the Y cutpoint fixed, we get results as in II, whereas the use of B as a cutpoint gives us figures such as those in III.

I		II		III	
2	48	0	50	25	25
48	2	25	25	50	0

Whether we get zero (or nearly zero) cells in one or both of two diagonally opposite cells depends on our choice of cutpoints.

To get data consistent with the proposition "X is both a necessary and a sufficient condition for Y," we should need to be fortunate in our choice of cutpoints.[7]   Unless all variables under consideration are best conceived theoretically as attributes, the use of "necessary and sufficient" terminology is deceptively simple.   It may work well for the logician but not the social scientist.   We shall return later to the use of attribute data.   In the meantime, we shall confine our discussion to continuous variables, with the recognition that attributes may at any time be treated as special cases, though sometimes troublesome ones.

The obvious objection to the proposed use of continuous variables is that most variables, while perhaps not best handled as attributes, cannot be measured with anywhere near the degree of accuracy to yield legitimate interval scales with clearly defined units of measurement.   Instead, we must deal with in-between situations: partially ordered scales, ordinal scales, or ordered metrics.[8]   Would it not, then, be more conservative to treat such data as attributes than to assume interval scales? Incidentally, this is essentially the position implied by the writer in an earlier work.[9]

Several comments are in order.   First, it is perhaps too early to estimate the relative seriousness of distortions produced by assuming interval scales, as compared with those introduced through the use of arbitrary cutpoints and crude categorization. Undoubtedly there will be different sets of circumstances under which the one or the other practice is preferable.   We have already noted that results may differ according to choice of cutpoints.   In addition, the use of dichotomized categories forces one to treat a distribution as bimodal in that all cases lumped into the "high" category are taken to have the same scores.   As

7. Notice that in this particular example, since the least squares line passes through the point $(\overline{X}, \overline{Y})$, if both variables were dichotomized near the medians and if the distributions were symmetrical, we would get a small number of cases in both cells of the diagonal.

8. See Coombs, "Social Measurement," for an excellent explanation of these various types of scales.

9. H. M. Blalock, *Social Statistics* (New York: McGraw-Hill Book Company, 1960), Chapter 2.

we shall see later, such a practice may lead to erroneous conclusions under certain kinds of conditions.

Secondly, we can admit that ideally it would be advantageous if we were to formulate our rationale so as to be appropriate for all levels of measurement, including intermediate levels involving ordinal scales. But unfortunately, relatively little attention has been given to these intermediate levels; the bulk of the literature on causal inferences seems to apply either to attribute data or to interval scales involving units of measurement.

In the present work, we cannot hope to fill this gap. Instead, we shall confine ourselves to a discussion of the rationale for interval scales, under the assumption that basically the same kind of rationale might be applied to lower levels of measurement. For example, this method will provide predictions about what should happen when we control for certain kinds of variables under a given causal model. In the absence of an alternative rationale in the case of ordinal scales, we can presume that ordinal techniques should yield similar conclusions under the identical causal model.

Finally, it may prove advantageous to *think* in terms of continuous variables, even where measurement is much more crude. The advantage over attribute thinking is that we may then always treat attributes as special cases of variables with only two values. On the other hand, if we think in terms of attributes and categoric logic, the transition to continuous variates is more difficult, though of course technically possible. Perhaps, however, this is a matter that depends on the training and intellectual background of the individual scholar, and it probably should not be insisted on too strongly.

INDEPENDENT AND DEPENDENT VARIABLES:
THE PROBLEM OF ASYMMETRY

As mentioned previously, mathematical systems may permit a good deal more flexibility than is allowed in experimental situations. In the present section we shall be concerned with an instance in which the terms "independent" and "dependent" variables are used somewhat differently in the language of mathematics than when we make use of causal terminology. Mathematical rules of operation usually allow for a certain type of symmetry between independent and dependent variables that our causal language may not permit.

In mathematics we conventionally mean by a "dependent variable" whatever variable happens to appear on the left-hand side of the equation. Thus if we write $Y = a + bX$ we are considering Y to be dependent and X independent. We say that Y is a "function" of X. But we recognize that we could just as easily have rewritten the equation as $X = -a/b + Y/b$, in which case X is taken as dependent. The two equations are algebraically equivalent and can be used interchangeably. In other words, we are ordinarily permitted to treat X and Y perfectly symmetrically.

Whether or not we wish to take X and Y as symmetrically related in a causal sense, however, is another matter. For some types of theoretical relationships we might consider that a change in X can cause a change in Y and vice versa. In such an instance, we need not be bothered by the mathematical interchange of X and Y. But, as argued previously, we might want to allow for the possibility that the causal relationship is basically asymmetrical: that a change in X can produce a change in Y, but not vice versa. For example, we might expect that a change in aptitudes or abilities might produce a change in performance, but that performance will not affect abilities.

As Wold and Jureen indicate, in experimental situations there is usually no ambiguity as to which variable one is taking as dependent and which independent.[10] One deliberately manipulates the independent variable physically in some way and observes the change in the dependent variable. In such instances the translation into mathematical notation is straightforward. The dependent variable in the causal sense is simply

10. Herman Wold and Lars Jureen, *Demand Analysis* (New York: John Wiley & Sons, 1953), pp. 31-32. This work contains an excellent general discussion of regression analysis applied to causal inferences. See especially Chapter 2.

placed on the left-hand side, and there are no ambiguities, and no real temptation to turn the equation around. But in non-experimental studies, where there is some doubt as to which variable to take as independent, we are not so sure. It might appear as though one could take either X or Y as independent, in both the causal and mathematical senses. But without being in a position actually to manipulate one or the other variable, we cannot tell whether a change in one of the variables will in fact produce a change in the other.

If we wish to use probability models that allow for the operation of variables other than those being explicitly considered, we must extend the notion of the perfect mathematical function to that of the regression equation that allows for error terms. In the case of linear models, if we write $Y = a + bX$ we are saying that Y (ideally) is a perfect function of X and that we can estimate Y scores exactly if we know the X values. All points will be exactly on the line. In such an instance, if we write X as the dependent variable, we get precisely the same mathematical relationship solved for X instead of Y.

When we introduce error terms, writing linear equations of the form

$$Y_i = a + bX_i + e_i,$$

the problem is no longer so simple. Scores are now scattered, and we can only attempt to find a straight line (or other curve) with an approximate fit. As is well known, there are several "best fitting" lines, depending on the nature of the criteria we wish to use. In particular we may find the lines that minimize the sums of the squared deviations in either the Y or X dimensions. If we take Y as dependent, we conceive of a regression of Y on X as a path of the mean Y scores for fixed values of X. We estimate the coefficients in such an equation by minimizing the sums of the squared deviations in the Y dimension. But if we take X as dependent, we find the line that minimizes the sum of squares in the X dimension.

When we allow for error terms the numerical values of the respective slopes b_{yx} and b_{xy} of the two least squares equations will *not* be exactly reciprocally related, but will be related by the equation $b_{yx}b_{xy} = r^2$. Only when r^2 is unity, i.e., when there is perfect prediction, will the two lines coincide. We have lost the complete reversibility that was possible in the case of the mathematical function. It now makes a difference which variable we take as dependent. How much of a difference it makes practically, or how different the two lines will be empirically, depends upon the amount of error involved.

But while the actual estimation equation we use depends upon our choice of dependent variable, the degree to which we can predict from the one variable to the other may be a symmetrical matter. *If we measure the accuracy of prediction in terms of the square of the correlation coefficient, then we may estimate Y scores just as accurately from X values as from the other way around.* The numerical value of r^2 tells us the percentage of the variation in either variable which is associated with the other. *In this sense, estimation is a symmetrical matter.*[11]

PREDICTION VERSUS CAUSAL INFERENCES

One way of dodging the problem of causality is to deal only with covariations and the notion of prediction. Thus one can ask how well we can predict from X to Y, or vice versa, while completely begging the question of the causal relationship between the two. The statistical literature, it seems, is almost schizophrenic in its approach to the question. While I have not made a systematic content analysis of the language used in various statistics texts and writings, there seems to be considerable confusion of terminology and almost a conspiracy of silence in dealing with the problem of causality.

The literature on experimental designs, on the one hand, is filled with causal terminology. One takes out the effects of control variables, studies interaction effects, and assigns individuals to "treatments." On the other hand, there seems to

11. There are, of course, various asymmetrical measures of association, values of which depend upon the choice of the variable to be predicted. In the present work, however, we shall confine our attention to product-moment correlations which are symmetrical.

be much less use of causal terminology in discussions of regression analysis, which are primarily handled in terms of prediction or estimation. Perhaps this difference in terminology reflects, in part, the influence of pioneers such as R. A. Fisher and Karl Pearson. Pearson, whose work on correlation and regression has been highly significant, was of course a member of the empiricist school of thought which rejected causal thinking, at least philosophically.[12]

Our present concern is not with experimental designs, which have limited applications in sociology and in other social sciences, but with techniques that are more appropriate for cross-sectional studies carried out at a single point in time, or perhaps at several points in time. The logic of experimental designs seems to be much more clearly understood, or at least does not seem to be surrounded with as much confusion as is the case when these ideal methods cannot be employed. Let us examine the kind of theoretical interpretation or way of looking at data which seems to characterize the nonexperimental statistical literature.

We are usually asked by the statistician to consider a situation in which there is a population of individuals with certain fixed characteristics. More often than not, we imagine different characteristics at a single point in time, although we might make use of data pertaining to different time periods. The time element, in other words, is not really crucial, though for simplicity we shall suppose that we have scores on each individual at a given point in time. To be specific, suppose we have three measures X, Y, and Z on each individual. We then treat this population as fixed but with unknown parameters (e.g., population means or correlation coefficients). A sample may be drawn from the population and estimates of these parameters made. Or one may test certain hypotheses concerning the values of these parameters.

Here, however, we shall focus our attention on the problem of prediction. A typical type of question asked by the statistician is, "How well can we predict an individual's score on one

12. Pearson, *The Grammar of Science*, Chapters 4 and 5.

variable, say Y, knowing his scores on the remaining variables?"
We imagine ourselves selecting an individual from this fixed
population, measuring him on X and Z, and then estimating
his Y score on the basis of (1) his own X and Z scores, and (2)
our knowledge of the joint frequency distributions of X, Y, and
Z. We may ask both what single value of Y we should predict
and how much faith we should have in this prediction. But we
do not ask about causal interrelationships among the three
variables.

We should note that a particular set of joint frequency distributions among variables such as X, Y, and Z could have been
obtained by any number of causal mechanisms. X may cause
Y, Y may cause X, there may be reciprocal causation, both X
and Y may be caused by Z, and so forth. The only information
we are given is the end result, namely a set of scores that are
interrelated in a fixed way. But although there may be a
number of different causal mechanisms which could all give rise
to the same end results, there are also a large number of causal
mechanisms which would *not* create these particular results.
In other words, *the population data will be consistent with certain
causal models but not others, and our task will be to find ways of
choosing among these alternative models on the basis of the population data*, in this case presumed to apply to a single point in time.

Let us illustrate with a simple example. Suppose the population scores for X, Y, and Z show that X is highly related to
Y and to Z, but that the relationship between Y and Z is much
weaker. By what causal mechanisms could this have come
about? Immediately, we shall have to make some simplifying
assumptions about other variables, but for the time being let
us merely assume that all other factors can be ignored. One
possibility is that X is a cause of both Y and Z but that there is
no direct link between the latter two variables. Another is
that Y caused X, which in turn caused Z, making X an intermediate link in the chain. But what if X caused Y, which in
turn caused Z? As we shall see later, this causal possibility
can be ruled out since it can be expected to result in a stronger
relationship between Y and Z than between X and Z.

Without some assumptions about the underlying causal mechanisms, we cannot deal with a very important type of problem. Suppose, for example, that we select an individual randomly from the population, measure his X and Z scores, and estimate his Y score from these values. We obtain the estimate, ideally, in the following way. We take all of the individuals with exactly the same scores on X and Z, and we use as our estimate the mean Y score of this group. But now suppose we ask, "What can we expect to happen to this individual's Y score if we were to change his X score while leaving his Z score the same?"

There is an ambiguity, here, as to what we mean by changing his X score. One meaning is as follows: we still imagine ourselves as dealing with a fixed population of scores, and therefore we are not at liberty to change any individual's score physically. However, we can imagine ourselves substituting another individual for the first. The second individual has the same Z score but a different X score, say one that is ten points higher. We then compare the expected Y scores on the two individuals and conclude that a "change" in X of ten units is associated with a change in Y of five units.

This is not the same sort of operational procedure, however, as actually manipulating the individual's properties so as to give him a really new X score. The first type of change involved a substitution of individuals or, if one prefers, a paper-and-pencil hypothetical manipulation. The second type involved a "forcing" or producing agent in the causal sense. The two are most certainly not operationally equivalent. Suppose, for example, that Y were a cause of X, though not the only one, but that a change in X will not produce a change in Y. Then if we can actually manipulate an individual in such a manner that his X score changes, we would not ordinarily expect a change in his Y score. But if we carry out the substitution or paper-and-pencil operation, when we select among individuals with higher X scores we can expect to find higher Y scores as well. Unfortunately, we would have reached the same conclusions in the case of the mathematical substitution regardless of whether X caused Y or Y caused X. This would not of course be true in the case of the physical "forcing" type of change.

There is thus a certain type of symmetry in the mathematical kind of "changing" which may not be appropriate for causal analyses. Perhaps it would be well to use different terminology in order to distinguish between the two types of operations. We would suggest the terms "substitution" or "shifting of scores" as appropriate for the mathematical operation, reserving the term "change" for an actual producing-mechanism type of operation.

It should be noted that the statistician usually uses the notion of prediction in the sense of "estimation." We assume that we are given the numerical values of one variable, say X, and asked to estimate or guess what the values of Y will be. We presume that all of the population data are fixed and that we are merely interested in how well a knowledge of one variable improves our ability to predict the other, over what we could accomplish without being given such a knowledge of the first variable. Suppose, for example, that X is education and Y income. Not knowing anything about a person's education, our best guess as to his income would be either the mean or median income of the entire group, depending on the criteria used. But if we knew his education, our best guess would then be the mean (or median) income for all persons having this *particular* education. We could then determine how much our guesses would be improved, given a knowledge of education, over our guesses without such a knowledge.

It should be perfectly apparent that the direction of causality is irrelevant in such estimation problems. We might just as well have been given the income data and asked to estimate the individual's education. We are saying that we could do equally well estimating education from income as the other way around. The problem involves a completely symmetrical relationship between X and Y.

But prediction may be used in another sense that is more closely connected to causal usage. Often, we wish to predict a future event from present characteristics. One may attempt to predict future performance in college on the basis of certain test information, for example. While one could just as readily estimate these scores from later performance, it is the scores that are known and not the performance. Whenever such predictions refer to future events, it is likely to be the case that the variable to be predicted (and for which scores are presently unknown) will be the one for which values are assigned only at the later of the two time periods. Where a causal relationship is involved, the *predicted* variable will undoubtedly be the *dependent* variable causally.

Thus, whereas the problems of prediction and establishing causal relationships are theoretically quite different, they are apt to be confused in practice. In order to avoid the ambiguity involved, we shall hereafter use the neutral term "estimation" in preference to "prediction," with the understanding that estimation is a symmetrical matter in which temporal sequences need not be involved. We recognize, however, that from the standpoint of practical goals (e.g., predicting performance in college), we are more likely to be interested in estimating the dependent variable from an independent variable, or a future event from present properties.

There are two distinct uses for regression equations, (1) *as estimating equations, and* (2) *as causal models.*[13] As Wold and

13. Wold and Jureen, *Demand Analysis,* p. 30. Perhaps we should make use of completely different terminology in the two cases. A lack of conceptual clarification seems in part responsible for the author's difference of opinion with William S. Robinson. See W. S. Robinson, "Asymmetric Causal Models: Comments on Polk and Blalock, "*American Sociological Review,* XXVII (August, 1962), 545-48. Robinson is bothered by the fact that we conceive of X as a cause of Y, and yet take X as caused only by outside variables. He finds it difficult to reconcile this with the symmetry involved in the notion of a bivariate or joint frequency distribution between X and Y. But as we have already noted, a bivariate (and normal) frequency distribution between X and Y could readily be generated by a causal mechanism in which variation in X is produced by other variables, with X in turn producing a portion of the variation in Y. To be sure, if we conceive of a fixed population, then the joint frequency distribution may have certain symmetrical qualities, making it equally justifiable to speak of Y's distributed about X's or X's about Y's. But we prefer to formulate models in

Jureen point out, the problem of estimation is relatively straight-forward and has been the subject of few theoretical controversies. Estimation is basically a matter of the state of the observer's knowledge; he is given certain pieces of information from which he wishes to make statements about unknown values. From here on, we shall be concerned with the second type of usage for regression equations, that involving causal laws. When we refer to estimation problems, we shall be considering only the question of estimating population parameters from sample statistics. Quite obviously, this is a different sort of problem from that in which we wish to estimate the value of some dependent variable from a combination of scores on other variables from the same sample.

For simplicity, we shall assume that causal relationships can be represented by linear regression models, though theoretically we can handle nonlinear relationships in a similar manner. Realistically, however, the more variables with which we must deal, and the more complex the causal model, the simpler our assumptions must be concerning the manner in which the variables are combined. We shall also assume that the effects of the several variables are additive, though we shall comment later on nonadditive models. In some cases it will be possible to change nonlinear or nonadditive models into linear additive ones by simple transformations (e.g., logarithmic transformations). In many instances, simple linear models will give close enough approximations for practical purposes.

OUTSIDE INFLUENCES, ERROR TERMS, AND CORRELATIONS

Presumably, a major goal in theory building is to make use of deductive types of arguments which at the same time go beyond common sense and yet which can be evaluated empirically. In the previous chapter we argued that in view of the present status of the social sciences it would seem highly advis-

terms of causal mechanisms that produce these joint frequency distributions, thereby allowing for asymmetry. As previously noted, however, we must recognize that several alternative causal mechanisms may generate the same set of joint frequencies. See also footnote 21 of this chapter.

able in actually constructing such theories—as well as in statistical tests of hypotheses—to allow for the influence of variables that have not been explicitly included in the theoretical system. We can always expect a certain amount of unexplained variation that in the limiting case may be reduced nearly to zero. Our aim is to make certain simplifying assumptions about outside influences which are sufficiently precise to allow for definite empirical predictions without being so highly restrictive as to permit tests only under the most ideal conditions.

The most restrictive assumptions are, of course, that outside influences are either actually nonexistent or that their effects are so small that they can be neglected or treated as minor measurement errors. If we are permitted such restrictive assumptions, we can avail ourselves of the use of categoric logic and mathematics (as contrasted with statistics). For example, in the case of attributes we can make assertions of the type, "If all A's are B's and if all B's are C's, then all A's will be C's." Or we may develop tidy linkages between variables, as in the statement, "If A implies B and if B implies C, then A implies C."

Another possibility is that we allow for errors and random variations but that we specify the amount of such variation, or perhaps some upper limit to this amount. For example, we might make statements of the form, "At least 80 per cent of the A's are B's," or "If A occurs, B will occur 80 per cent of the time," or, alternatively, "The probability of B, given A, is .80." It might then be possible to make a series of assertions about the relative frequency with which two variables, indirectly connected by a third, should be associated. But if we were unable to specify such probabilities a priori, and if we found it necessary to substitute vague expressions such as "If A occurs B will *usually* occur," then it would become extremely difficult to develop deductive systems that go very far beyond the common-sense level. For example, it would not necessarily be correct to assert, "If A then usually B, and if B then usually C; therefore if A then usually C." The alternative "If A then sometimes C" might be more sensible, but it would hardly be very enlightening.

Clearly, we will seldom be in a position theoretically to say anything very exact about the absolute amount of error and unexplained variation that is produced by variables that have not even been identified, let alone measured. Empirically, we can perhaps determine the absolute amount of unexplained variation, but this will most certainly be relative to the particular situation and will therefore have very little general significance. It is for this reason that *correlation coefficients, which in effect measure the amount of unexplained variation, have little or no theoretical significance in themselves, though they may be used to test the adequacy of any given causal model.* This particular point will be emphasized later in a number of connections.

If we cannot hope to specify theoretically the amounts of error involved, or the relative proportion of times, say, that A and B will be found together, then exactly what kinds of assumptions about unexplained variation can we make? Instead of attempting to specify how much disturbance is created by outside variables, we can concentrate on *how* they are operating. For example, are the variations produced essentially random, no matter how large? If not random, are the unexplained variations in one variable in any way related to the remaining variables that have been explicitly included?

Assumptions About Error Terms. Let us suppose we are dealing with a single dependent variable Y and a number of "independent" variables X_i. *We shall have to assume that whatever outside variables are operating on Y are creating variation that is completely unrelated to that produced by any of the X_i.* This might occur under either of two circumstances.

First, there may be a large number of outside causes of Y, no one of which has very great influence. Any one of these minor causes might be related to one or more of the X_i, but if so its possible disturbing influences would have to be counterbalanced by certain of the other outside variables. For example, a given outside variable might be positively correlated with both X_1 and Y. But another might be positively related to Y but negatively to X_1, so that the net effect of the two disturbances is to cancel each other out in the sense that the total variation in Y produced by both variables is unrelated to the variation in X_1.

Secondly, and perhaps more realistically, we may admit that unexplained variation in Y is produced primarily by one or two major factors in addition to a large number of minor ones. But if so, then these major factors cannot be related to any of the X_i which have been explicitly considered. What if there existed a major determinant of Y, not explicitly contained in the regression equation, which was in fact correlated with some of the independent variables X_i? Clearly, it would be contributing to the error term in a manner so as to make the errors systematically related to these particular X_i. If we were in a position to bring this unknown variable into the regression equation, we would find that at least some of the regression coefficients (slopes) would be changed.[14] This is obviously an unsatisfactory state of affairs, making it nearly impossible to state accurate scientific generalizations. For if we can change the values of the coefficients almost at will by the addition of new variables, then how can any causal laws be established?

We shall also wish to discuss models in which there is more than one dependent variable. For each variable we wish to take as dependent on some other variable, it will be necessary to assume that outside causes of this variable produce variation which is independent of that produced by any of the explicitly listed causes. Practically, this will ordinarily require us to make the same kinds of assumptions as were necessary in the case of a single dependent variable. We may imagine a large number of minor outside causes of each variable, the net effect of these outside factors being the production of random variation in each of the variables in the explicit causal system. Or we can allow for the influence of one or two major outside causes of each variable, provided we assume that the causes of any one variable are unrelated to those of any other. For example, we may take the outside variables U and V as major causes of X

14. Wold and Jureen, *Demand Analysis*, pp. 37-38. These authors point out that it is theoretically possible to change a given slope to any finite value, positive or negative, with the introduction of the proper additional variable.

and Y, respectively, but we must then assume that U and V are completely independent. *Obviously, then, we must assume that there is no single major cause of more than one variable. If U causes both X and Y, then such a variable must be brought into the system if erroneous inferences are to be avoided.*

There will obviously be any number of possible variables that are correlated with each of the independent variables X_i. Particularly likely is the situation in which the investigator has a number of measures or indicators of what he considers to be the same underlying theoretical variable. If all such measures are highly intercorrelated, he may merely select the one measure that he considers most appropriate, or he may combine these indicators into a composite index that, presumably, is considered a better measure of the underlying variable. But if he makes use of all of his indicators as distinct variables in the regression equation, he may have considerable difficulty in interpreting his results theoretically, though he may improve his ability to *estimate* the dependent variable.

The set of variables that will be most appropriate for a causal regression equation is therefore not necessarily the same set that will be best for estimation purposes. It is suggested that where causal inferences are desired, the investigator be careful to select variables that are presumed to be causally interrelated in rather clear-cut ways (e.g., education and job opportunities) and to avoid the use (as distinct variables) of indices that are thought to be measures of the "same" underlying variable. More will be said in Chapter V concerning the use of unmeasured variables in causal models, but for the time being we shall assume that each variable that appears in the regression equation represents the actual variable about which one wishes to make causal inferences.

To return to the problem of error terms, we must assume, then, that errors in Y are essentially irregular and unrelated to any of the independent variables X_i, and that any variable that is a major cause of the dependent variable Y and at the same time is correlated with any of the X_i has been explicitly brought into the causal model. But how can we test such an assumption? Unfortunately we cannot do so unless we have been able to investigate the behavior of the error terms through replication. And in nonexperimental studies this is usually not possible.

Apparently our only alternative is to search for possible disturbing influences and to bring them explicitly into the causal picture. In so doing, of course, we are transforming type 4 confounding variables into type 2 variables that can be brought under control. But at some point we must stop and make the simplifying assumption that the effects of the remaining confounding influences are so negligible that they can be safely ignored. It is always the privilege of the critic to point to disturbing influences that we have omitted or failed to measure. By bringing these variables explicitly into the picture, he can then make use of a more complex model to see if he can make superior predictions for other data. In such a manner, scientific knowledge accumulates.

One further point about error terms should be noted. In any realistic situation there will always be at least two very different types of errors. First, there will be measurement errors. *Ordinary regression analysis is usually based upon the assumption that there may be errors of measurement with respect to the dependent variable Y, but that all of the independent variables have been measured without error.* Such an assumption is obviously unrealistic in the case of most social science data.

Secondly, we assume that "errors" in Y may be owing to the effects of outside variables that have not been brought explicitly into the causal model. The type of model we have been discussing allows for this second type of error. Other types of regression models allow for measurement errors in all variables but make the assumptions that we have been able to include all relevant variables in the model and that measurement errors are the only errors involved.[15]

Unfortunately, relatively simple mathematical procedures for models that combine both types of errors do not seem to have been developed. And in addition, we usually have no effective

15. *Ibid.*, pp. 38-42.

ways in nonexperimental studies of assessing the relative magnitudes of the errors due to these two sources.   We shall have to assume for the present that measurement errors are very slight as compared with errors or variation produced by outside influences.   Measurement errors will be considered in somewhat greater detail in Chapter V.

Slopes Versus Correlations.   Sociologists and psychologists are much more accustomed to thinking in terms of correlation coefficients, or other measures of *degree* of relationship, than in terms of regression coefficients or slopes.   The reasons are not difficult to determine.   With crude measurement procedures and a shortage of variables that can legitimately be measured as interval scales, the exact size of the slope has little real meaning. Furthermore, measures have not been sufficiently standardized from one study to the next to make comparisons of slopes very meaningful.   Two investigators may measure urbanization in different ways, making it difficult to attach a consistent meaning to the magnitudes of any slopes they may obtain when relating urbanization to some other variable, which would also undoubtedly be measured differently in the two studies.   A comparison of the correlation coefficients, however, would seem to make more sense.   At the very least, correlations always vary between the same two limits and can be interpreted in terms of proportion of variation "explained."

Also, social scientists are primarily engaged at present in merely locating variables that they think will be important. The magnitudes of the error terms, or "unexplained" variations, are so large as to make accurate estimates of regression coefficients difficult and perhaps premature.   In view of all this, why give so much attention to regression coefficients?

As we shall see later, the behavior of correlation coefficients leaves a good deal to be desired in comparative studies.   The fact that correlations always vary between -1 and $+1$ provides them with a property which is deceptively disarming.   This can readily be seen when we realize that the proportion of variation "explained" is not only a function of the inherent nature of the relationship between the independent and dependent variables, but also of the degree to which *other* variables have been brought under control.

In experimental situations the investigator deliberately attempts to control for as many extraneous factors as possible. Through manipulations of various kinds, he also tries to give the independent variable sufficient variation so that it will explain a high proportion of the variation in *Y*. In other words, he attempts to maximize the correlation by reducing the effects of extraneous factors while at the same time maximizing the effects of the independent variable under study. Clearly, it is not the size of the correlation coefficient, per se, in which he is inherently interested. A large correlation merely means a low degree of scatter about the least squares equation and hence an accurate estimate of the true slope. The size of the correlation coefficient tells him how successful he is being in attaining his real goal, namely in describing the *nature* of the relationship between his variables. *It is the regression coefficients which give us the laws of science.*

Ideally, then, our attention should be focused on slopes rather than on correlation coefficients. However, there are several instances in which we may legitimately be interested in the *r*'s themselves. The first is in situations where we expect a correlation to disappear. Since the vanishing of a correlation coefficient is equivalent to the comparable slope's being equal to zero, we may in this special case work directly with the correlations.[16] As will be seen in the next chapter, a method for inferring causal relationships from correlational data, introduced by Herbert Simon, involves sets of predictions from causal models where certain combinations of correlations can be expected to disappear.

16. John W. Tukey argues that the use of correlation coefficients in preference to slopes is justified only under two principal conditions: when exact measurement is hopeless or when slopes and correlations are numerically the same. See John W. Tukey, "Causation, Regression and Path Analysis," in Oscar Kempthorne, *et al.*, *Statistics and Mathematics in Biology* (Ames, Iowa: Iowa State College Press, 1954), Chapter 3. We should note that we are here dealing with an instance in which slopes and correlations reduce to the same value, namely zero.

Another instance in which our focus of attention should legitimately be placed on the magnitude of correlation coefficients is where we wish to assess the relative importance of different variables in some specific situation involving *actual* changes. Regression equations give us abstract laws that tell us how much one variable should change *if* a given variable changes by a particular amount. They deal only with hypothetical changes, which may or may not take place.

Two variables may be causally related in the abstract, but if the independent variable does not vary in a particular instance, it cannot be considered "important" as a cause. Some other variable, connected to the dependent variable by a slope that is much less steep, may be a much more important cause than the first because of the fact that in this *particular* instance its value happened to change considerably. In assessing relative importance, we need to know *how much* a given independent variable varies and *what proportion* of the variation in the dependent variable it explains, either directly or indirectly.

THE USE OF SIMULTANEOUS EQUATIONS

For the most part we have been assuming that there is a single dependent variable Y and a number of supposedly independent variables X_i. The magnitudes of the regression coefficients give the expected change in Y for a given change in one of the independent variables, *assuming that the remaining independent variables are held constant*. Such a single equation is indeed appropriate in experimental studies in which the investigator can study the relationship of the dependent variable to each independent variable, taken separately. We imagine his being in a position to hold the control variables literally constant. The hypothetical question, "What happens to Y if we were to change only one of the X_i's?" has a direct counterpart in experimental manipulations.

But what about nonexperimental situations in which we cannot hold all variables constant but one? In particular, suppose some of the X_i's are causes of others. When a given X_i changes, not only will there be a direct effect upon Y, but there may be an indirect one as well through the operation of other variables that also change as a result of the original change in X_i. In real-life situations, we certainly recognize the existence of more than one dependent variable, and we must somehow or another develop a mathematical model that represents this fact.

Econometricians have become accustomed to dealing with complex causal systems involving large numbers of variables under nonexperimental conditions. A common solution is to make use of entire sets of simultaneous equations, which are referred to as "structural systems."[17] The literature on structural systems is becoming fairly extensive and is highly technical, but we shall attempt to deal with only a limited number of issues discussed in nontechnical terminology.

Having selected a given set of variables, we can write a separate equation for each variable as a possible dependent variable. Referring to the variables as $X_1, X_2, \ldots, X_k$ and dropping the letter Y since we no longer have a single dependent variable, we may write such equations as follows:

$$X_1 = a_1 + b_{12}X_2 + b_{13}X_3 + \ldots + b_{1k}X_k + e_1$$
$$X_2 = a_2 + b_{21}X_1 + b_{23}X_3 + \ldots + b_{2k}X_k + e_2$$
$$\vdots$$
$$X_k = a_k + b_{k1}X_1 + b_{k2}X_2 + \ldots + b_{k,k-1}X_{k-1} + e_k.$$

We are admitting the possibility that each of the X_i may be caused by all of the remaining variables. The e_i refer to the effects of all outside variables on the appropriate dependent variables. *But unless we can make certain simplifying assumptions to the effect that some of the b's are zero, we shall run into difficulties in estimating the various coefficients.* Only under special conditions will the coefficients be "identifiable" in the sense that they will have unique values.[18] Likewise, we cannot

17. Wold and Jureen, *Demand Analysis*, pp. 48-57.

18. For discussions of the problem of identifiability, see W. C. Hood and T. C. Koopmans (eds.), *Studies in Econometric Method* (New York: John Wiley & Sons, 1953). See also J. Johnston, *Econometric Methods* (New York: McGraw-Hill Book Company, 1963), Chapter 9.

generally use ordinary least squares procedures to give us unbiased estimates of these coefficients.[19]

Our concern will be with a certain subclass of structural
systems which are referred to as recursive. An example of a
recursive system would be one in which we rule out two-way
causation. If a particular X_i is taken as a cause of X_j, then X_j
cannot cause X_i. In terms of the slopes, this means that some
of the b's must be set equal to zero, and in particular if $b_{ij} \neq 0$,
then b_{ji} must be zero. By renumbering the variables it will
then be possible to write the set of equations as follows:

$$X_1 = e_1$$
$$X_2 = b_{21}X_1 + e_2$$
$$X_3 = b_{31}X_1 + b_{32}X_2 + e_3$$
$$\cdot$$
$$\cdot$$
$$\cdot$$
$$X_k = b_{k1}X_1 + b_{k2}X_2 + \ldots + b_{k,k-1}X_{k-1} + e_k.$$

Here, we have also gotten rid of the constant terms by assuming
that each variable is measured in terms of deviations from its
mean.

We are now taking X_1 to be independent of all the rest. Its
value is determined only by variables that are outside the causal
system. It is what econometricians call an "exogenous" variable. But X_2 depends not only on outside variables but on X_1 as
well. In turn, X_3 depends on X_1 and X_2 but not on any of the
remaining explicitly defined variables. Finally, X_k depends on
all of the remaining X_i.

The regression coefficients are seen to take on a triangular
form, with half of the b's having been set equal to zero. In any
particular model, we may also set some of the remaining b's

19. Wold and Jureen, *Demand Analysis*, pp. 49-52. See also Trygve Haavelmo, "The Statistical Implications of a System of Simultaneous Equations,"
Econometrica, XI (January, 1943), 1-12. In essence, simple least squares procedures break down for structural equations involving reciprocal causation
owing to the fact that error terms can no longer be assumed to be uncorrelated
with the independent variables in each equation. Under certain circumstances
the biases involved may be quite serious.

equal to zero. For example, if b_{21} is zero, then X_2 does not depend upon X_1, and we have two exogenous variables that are caused only by outside factors. As we shall see later on, whenever we set one of these remaining b's equal to zero, we expect some total or partial correlation to be zero, and we can use this fact to obtain a set of prediction equations for evaluating any particular causal model in terms of correlational data.

Recursive systems have an important property that is not generally true of structural systems. We can make use of ordinary least squares procedures to estimate the various nonzero coefficients, and our estimates will be unbiased.[20] This means, practically, that the slopes can be estimated from sample data by means of the usual formulas given in elementary texts. But it must be kept in mind that if we allow for two-way causation, so that it is possible that both b_{ij} and b_{ji} are nonzero, then the problem of estimating the slopes is considerably more complex. A failure to recognize this fact may lead one to assume that two equations are actually inconsistent when in fact they are not.[21] Thus if ordinary least squares were generally used to estimate both b_{ij} and b_{ji}, we could expect the two estimates of the slopes to vanish at once (when $r_{ij} = 0$), which would appear to be inconsistent with the possibility that $b_{ij} \neq 0$ but $b_{ji} = 0$.

Reciprocal Causation. Recursive systems can actually be used to handle instances in which we imagine causation to be reciprocal, provided we are in a position to "lag" some of the variables. Empirically, in order to assess the adequacy of any

20. Wold and Jureen, *Demand Analysis*, pp. 51-52. For a later and more technical discussion of this topic by Wold, see R. H. Strotz and H. O. A. Wold, "A Triptych on Causal Systems," *Econometrica*, XXVIII (April, 1960), 417-63.

21. Both Kenneth Polk and W. S. Robinson, in discussing the simultaneous equation approach, apparently fail to make the distinction between least squares estimates and a regression equation appropriate to a population. Robinson, in attempting to show an apparent inconsistency in the method, presumably assumes that least squares estimates can legitimately be used as unbiased estimates of the parameters. See Robinson, "Asymmetric Causal Models," equation 3b, p. 547. Haavelmo ("Simultaneous Equations," *Econometrica*) shows that such an assumption cannot legitimately be made in the case of general structural equations. See also K. Polk, "A Note on Asymmetric Causal Models," *American Sociological Review*, XXVII (August, 1962), 539-42.

given causal model involving such lagged variables, we must be able to collect data at several points in time, and furthermore, the time intervals involved must coincide with some "natural" period of time. Since social scientists are seldom in a position to collect such data, we need only note the possibility of dealing with two-way causation in this manner. A few simple illustrations will suffice for our purposes.

Wold and Jureen provide a model in which demand at time t is assumed to be caused by prices at that same time.[22] The *supply* of goods at time t, however, is assumed caused by the prices at time $t-1$. Finally, the prices at time t are caused partly by the difference between demand and supply at time $t-1$. In order to collect data to provide a test for such a model, we would have to determine the time period (perhaps a full year) for which decisions of the producers to change production levels could be put into effect.

Taking a sociological example, we recognize a certain kind of reciprocal causation between the amount of minority job discrimination at a given point in time and educational achievement. We say that a Negro's job potential is determined by his education. On the other hand, educational aspirations may be affected by the existing level of job discrimination at that time. We might say that educational aspirations of a Negro youth at time t are caused by (perceived) job differentials at that same time t. But at some later time $t + 1$, when the youth has matured and entered the labor force, his job opportunities at $t+1$ depend upon his educational achievements at time t. By treating the same variables at different time periods as though they were distinct, the problem can be handled in terms of recursive equations. Thus certain variables at time $t-1$ may be taken as exogenous or independent, while these same variables at time t may be considered to be causally dependent on some of the other variables.

It will of course not always be appropriate to make use of recursive systems of equations. Probably most persons would agree that A cannot be a cause of B and B simultaneously a

22. Wold and Jureen, *Demand Analysis*, pp. 12-13.

cause of A. Yet we may wish to speak of X and Y being "mutual causes," or we allow for "reciprocal" causation. What we usually mean would be something like this: a change in X produces a change in Y, which in turn produces a further change in X at some later time, which produces a still further change in Y, and so on. Symbolically

$$X_{t_0} \rightarrow Y_{t_1} \rightarrow X_{t_2} \rightarrow Y_{t_3} \rightarrow X_{t_4} \rightarrow \ldots$$

An increase in the level of unemployment might lead to fewer retail sales at a somewhat later time. This, in turn, could lead to further unemployment, and so on.

Such instances of reciprocal causation can be handled by means of recursive equations provided data are collected at sufficiently frequent intervals. But what if the feedback is more or less "instantaneous" relative to the length of the intervals between data collections? For example, suppose data were collected only at times t_0, t_2, and t_4. Which way would we write the arrows? Perhaps the most reasonable procedure would be to make use of a set of structural equations which is not recursive and which permits one to assume that X can be a cause of Y and also Y a cause of X. As pointed out above, we shall then run into special difficulties, including the possibility that the coefficients cannot be uniquely identified or least squares estimates legitimately used. Discussion of such problems is well beyond the scope of the present work. The interested reader is referred, however, to some of the econometrics literature cited previously.

The Problem of Equivalent Sets of Equations. Mathematics, at times, allows for entirely too much flexibility. This is of course a major advantage of the mathematical language, but it sometimes makes translation difficult. It is as though one language has three words for the same concept whereas a second language has only one. In translating from the first language into the second, we face no real decisions, but when moving in the other direction we must choose among three alternatives. To illustrate the problem let us consider the three sets of simultaneous equations

$$X = 5$$
$$X + Y = 6 \quad \Big\} \quad (1)$$

$$X - Y = 4$$
$$X + Y = 6 \quad \Big\} \quad (2)$$

$$X = 5$$
$$Y = 1 \quad \Big\} \quad (3).$$

Although most of us have been trained to consider the last set as the solution to either (1) or (2), this third set can obviously be taken as a set of simultaneous equations in its own right, though we might wish to consider it almost trivial. The difficulty, here, is that all three sets are entirely equivalent mathematically. Indeed, we could find an infinite number of sets of equations all of which have these same solutions.

Notice that set (1) is of the recursive form, whereas (2) is an example of the more general structural form. Finally, (3) is put in a form that would imply X and Y to be causally independent. How can this be? The answer is that the equations are equivalent, *given these particular values of the coefficients and constant terms*. But suppose an "experimenter" were permitted to change some of these coefficients in each case. Let us now see what would happen in each of the three sets.

In set (1) if we could change *only* the first equation (say by changing the constant term to 4), then it is clear that we would affect both X and Y (now $X = 4$ and $Y = 2$). But suppose we were to change the constant in the second equation (say to 8). We would then change the value of Y (to 3) *but we would not affect X*. Considering next the second set, it is obvious that if we were to change the constant in *either* equation we would change *both* X and Y. Set (2) has a certain symmetry to it that set (1) does not. Finally, we note that for set (3) a change in the first equation affects *only* X, while a change in the second affects *only* Y. We can change either value without affecting the other.

Herbert Simon makes use of this difference in the properties of the three sets of equations to develop a formal definition of causal ordering.[23] There is no need to go into his argument in detail since it is quite technical. In essence he identifies causal orderings with sets of equations which are in a form similar to set (1). He reasons that simultaneous equations expressed in such a recursive form have a definite counterpart in the experimental situation. The experimenter or "nature" is in a position to change the values of the coefficients or constants in one equation at a time, though he cannot change a nonzero slope to zero, or vice versa. It would not be permissible to change a given slope to zero because this would imply the ability to make a causal relationship noncausal (or vice versa).

Recursive systems have the property that the experimenter can, by entering at a particular point, change only the values of whatever X_i *happen to appear at that point or below*, whereas more general structural equations do not have this property. Thus in the equations

$$X_1 = e_1$$
$$X_2 = b_{21}X_1 + e_2$$
$$X_3 = b_{31}X_1 + b_{32}X_2 + e_3$$
$$X_4 = b_{41}X_1 + b_{42}X_2 + b_{43}X_3 + e_4$$

a change in e_1 will affect all X's, a change in e_2 will affect X_2, X_3, and X_4 but not X_1, and a change in e_4 will produce a change only in X_4. In other words, if we manipulate outside variables that cause only X_4, we cannot affect any of the other variables.

The objective in limiting ourselves to recursive systems, even though there are other possible sets of equations with the same formal mathematical properties, is to reduce the flexibility of our mathematical system so as to coincide more realistically with experimental models in which a simple causal ordering is presumed. Where such an ordering cannot legitimately be assumed, the use of such recursive systems will of course not be appropriate.

There is never any guarantee that any particular use of mathematical reasoning will lead to conclusions that make sense when translated back into other theoretical languages. We shall see, however, that these recursive systems not only in-

23. Simon, *Models of Man*, Chapter 1.

volve relatively simple computational routines but—perhaps more important—they also lead to predictions about correlation coefficients and rules for controlling under various causal models that are entirely consistent with common sense. Yet they also enable us to go beyond the all too simple three-variable case that is commonly discussed in the literature.

In the final analysis, the degree to which one is satisfied with the conclusions derived by mathematical procedures depends on the way the translation has been made between the two theoretical languages. In attempting to discuss this very complex problem in layman's terminology, we have tended to oversimplify the basic issues involved. But there is a more technical literature available for those who care to delve into the matter more deeply.

III

Evaluating Causal Models

In the present chapter we shall discuss a procedure for evaluating the adequacy of specific causal models. The initial discussion will be rather abstract. For those who prefer to think in terms of concrete variables and realistic social science examples, we shall later consider two empirical applications, one involving anthropological data on North American Indian tribes and the other involving census data dealing with minority discrimination. In the former case, concern will be centered on the problem of inferring evolutionary sequences among the following variables: (1) division of labor, (2) residence patterns, (3) land tenure, and (4) systems of descent. The reader may therefore find it helpful to think concretely in terms of these specific variables instead of X_1, X_2, X_3, and X_4. Or he may prefer to make use of factors such as per cent urban, per cent nonwhite, white median incomes, and nonwhite median incomes since these particular variables will also be discussed at a later point. Alternatively, some readers may wish merely to skim the next two sections and to return to these materials after examining the specific applications.

RATIONALE FOR TESTING MODELS

It is quite correct that one can never demonstrate causality from correlational data, or in fact from any type of empirical information.   Nevertheless it is possible to make causal *inferences* concerning the adequacy of causal models, at least in the sense that we can proceed by eliminating inadequate models that make predictions that are not consistent with the data. As we have seen, such causal models involve (1) a finite set of explicitly defined variables, (2) certain assumptions about how these variables are interrelated causally, and (3) assumptions to the effect that outside variables, while operating, do not have confounding influences that disturb the causal patterning among the variables explicitly being considered.   We shall now discuss how such assumptions can be used to make predictions concerning intercorrelations, thus providing empirical criteria for evaluating the adequacy of the causal model in question.

Let us begin by rewriting the coefficients of a recursive system in a manner that is in keeping with conventional notation for regression coefficients.[1]   We shall assume that each variable has been measured in terms of deviations about its mean, so that we can omit the constant terms without loss of generality. Subscripts for the b's indicate the variables being held constant in any given case.   As before, we shall suppose that the variables have been labeled in such a way that X_1 is causally prior to the other variables, X_2 is prior to all variables except X_1, and so forth.   Confining ourselves to four variables, we can then write a recursive system as follows:

1. We have deliberately not made use of the conventional "dot notation" for partial slopes in our discussion up to this point.   This is partly for the sake of convenience, but it is also because we wish to emphasize that the familiar formulas, given in applied statistics texts, for partial slopes and correlations are not appropriate for all types of simultaneous equations.   In the case of recursive equations, however, the reader may apply these formulas to the coefficients of each equation taken separately.   We shall continue to use b's throughout, rather than beta's, since there will generally be no tendency to confuse population parameters with their sample estimates.   In situations where subscripts might be confusing, we shall shift to a notation using W, X, Y, and Z rather than X_1, X_2, . . . X_k.

$$X_1 = e_1 \tag{1}$$
$$X_2 = b_{21}X_1 + e_2 \tag{2}$$
$$X_3 = b_{31.2}X_1 + b_{32.1}X_2 + e_3 \tag{3}$$
$$X_4 = b_{41.23}X_1 + b_{42.13}X_2 + b_{43.12}X_3 + e_4 \tag{4}$$

Notice that in the equation for X_2, the slope b_{21} does not involve any controls for the remaining variables since these variables do not appear explicitly in the equation. Likewise there are no controls for X_4 in the third equation, although each of the slopes $b_{31.2}$ and $b_{32.1}$ involves a control for the remaining variable that appears in the equation. The last equation contains slopes with controls for two variables. Generally, there will be no controls for any variables that have not appeared in a given equation or any of the equations that are prior to it. In effect, this means that we do not control for dependent variables. In the above set of equations we can analyze the first three equations without reference to the fourth, but we cannot analyze the fourth causally without considering the first three. This property of recursive systems has important implications that will be discussed shortly.

If we are willing to assume the correctness of the above recursive causal model, we can estimate each of the b's by ordinary least squares. In order to do so we merely study each equation separately, estimating the b's by whatever standard computing routine is most convenient. But we are seldom in a theoretical position to make an out and out assumption that a given model is in fact correct. Instead, we wish to *test* the adequacy of the model in some way.

Unfortunately, however, we cannot make a simple test unless we impose certain additional restrictions on the model. Without these restrictions, we will find that we have the same number of unknowns as equations, so that each b can be estimated uniquely, regardless of the data. In order to provide a test of the model we must have fewer unknowns than equations, thereby imposing some conditions that the equations must satisfy in order for them to be mutually consistent. If the data are such that the equations are not mutually consistent, then we shall be in a position to reject the model as inadequate.

As Simon points out, the error terms as well as the b's will generally be unknown.[2] But if we can assume these errors to be uncorrelated we can obtain an additional set of equations that, together with the original set of recursive equations, will give us exactly the same number of equations as unknowns. If we now assume that one or more of the b's are equal to zero, we shall have fewer unknowns than equations. Generally, these equations will not be consistent. This means that the model in question will not work with all empirical data. For each b that is set equal to zero, we will have an additional equation over and above the number of unknowns. Thus if three of the b's of a recursive system are assumed to be zero, then there will be three such equations left over, equations that will be consistent with the others only under special conditions.

We can look upon these excess equations as "prediction equations" which should hold true if the model under study is actually appropriate. While the practical uses of such equations may not be evident until we have actually applied the method to several specific models, we can at least indicate the form that these equations will take. Keeping in mind that the numerators of correlation coefficients and slopes have the same values, we see that the vanishing of any given b is equivalent to the disappearance of the comparable partial correlation. It turns out that *the prediction equations can therefore be written in the form of some partial correlation set equal to zero*.

It has been indicated that each of the slopes involves controls for all variables that appear in any given equation, or in prior equations, but not for variables that appear only in later equations. Thus in equation (2) the slope b_{21} does not involve controls for either X_3 or X_4, which are dependent on X_1 and X_2. But $b_{31.2}$ does involve a control for X_2, and $b_{41.23}$ is a partial slope with controls on both X_2 and X_3. If we were to set $b_{21} = 0$, thereby indicating no direct link between X_1 and X_2,

2. Herbert A. Simon, *Models of Man* (New York: John Wiley & Sons, 1957), pp. 41-42. It should be noted that we are explicitly assuming that $E\,(e_i e_j) = 0$, for all $i \neq j$. This is in keeping with the assumption that outside variables have only random disturbing effects.

then we impose the condition that r_{12} should be zero, subject of course to sampling errors. This equation, i.e., $r_{12} = 0$, is the additional equation that must be approximately satisfied in order for the data to be consistent with the model in which there is no direct link between X_1 and X_2.

If we were to set $b_{31.2} = 0$, under the assumption that there is no direct link between X_1 and X_3, then $r_{13.2}$ should be approximately zero. Likewise the setting of $b_{41.23} = 0$ would imply that $r_{14.23}$ should be zero. Several of the b's may of course be set equal to zero simultaneously. For example if both b_{21} and $b_{31.2}$ are zero, then we shall obtain the two prediction equations $r_{12} = 0$ and $r_{13.2} = 0$. If we were to assume no direct links between X_1 and X_3, X_2 and X_4, and X_3 and X_4, then three of the correlations should be approximately zero. In this case the prediction equations would be (1) $r_{13.2} = 0$, (2) $r_{24.13} = 0$, and (3) $r_{34.12} = 0$. As we shall presently see, whenever several arrows have been erased certain simplifications may occur. These simplifications will take the form of the disappearance of one or more *lower-order* partials.

SPECIFIC CAUSAL MODELS

It will perhaps be most helpful at this point to turn to a number of particular causal models in order to illustrate the general rules. We can begin with the four-variable model in which all causal arrows are present, as in Figure 3. We are ruling out two-way causation and are making use of the recursive equations (1) through (4). We shall now eliminate arrows one by one, noting the nature of the resulting prediction equations. There are, of course, a large number of possible four-variable models, even presupposing this particular ordering among variables. Here it will be sufficient to examine only a relatively small number of special cases in order to indicate the general principles involved.[3]

Let us first eliminate the arrow between X_1 and X_3, as in Fig-

3. The four-variable case is discussed somewhat more thoroughly in H. M. Blalock, "Four-Variable Causal Models and Partial Correlations," *American Journal of Sociology*, LXVIII (September, 1962), 182-94.

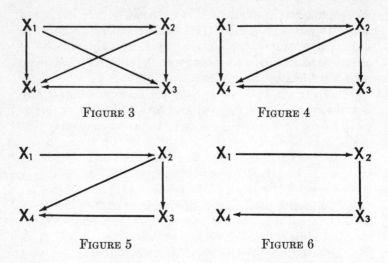

FIGURE 3

FIGURE 4

FIGURE 5

FIGURE 6

ure 4, giving us the prediction equation $r_{13.2} = 0$.   This says that when we control for the intervening variable X_2, the partial between X_1 and X_3 should be approximately zero.   In an experimental situation we would say that *if* it were possible to hold X_2 constant, while still varying X_1, there should be no change in the mean value of X_3.   In order to hold X_2 constant when one of its causes (X_1) varied, we would have to manipulate some other causes of X_2 in such a manner as to counteract exactly the changes in X_1.   Ordinarily we would not carry out such a controlling operation in experimental designs, although theoretically it would be possible to do so.

Suppose we were to consider what would happen if we also introduced a control for X_4, the dependent variable.   Experimentally, of course, we would never be tempted to control in this manner.   But one of the very real disadvantages of mathematical manipulations, as contrasted with those in the laboratory, is in the extreme flexibility they permit.   There is certainly nothing in the formulas for partial correlations which would prohibit our controlling for X_4, nor would there be any rules of thumb for judging whether or not the numerical results were sufficiently absurd to rule out such a control. This decision can only be made in terms of the particular model we have postulated.

If one were to control for X_4 under this particular model, then whereas $r_{13.2}$ should be zero, the value of $r_{13.24}$ should not ordinarily vanish. This can easily be seen from the formula

$$r_{13.24} = \frac{r_{13.2} - r_{14.2}r_{34.2}}{\sqrt{1 - r^2_{14.2}}\,\sqrt{1 - r^2_{34.2}}} .$$

Clearly, if $r_{13.2}$ is zero, the only way that $r_{13.24}$ can also be zero is for either $r_{14.2}$ or $r_{34.2}$ to vanish. Since this will not generally happen in the case of the model of Figure 4, we conclude that an additional control for the dependent variable X_4 ordinarily gives a nonvanishing partial.

We must therefore introduce a note of caution. *The phrase "controlling for all relevant variables" does not mean that one should automatically control for all variables that might be available to the researcher, including possible dependent variables.* It means that one should control only for variables that are either prior to one or both of the variables being related or that may be intervening between them. Even this rule can give misleading results depending upon the purposes of one's investigation. But at the very least, we can indicate that one should not control for dependent variables.

Suppose that we next erase the arrow between X_1 and X_4, giving us a model in which X_1 is only an indirect cause of X_4 by way of X_2, which itself is both a direct and an indirect cause of X_4. (See Figure 5.) We have now the two prediction equations $r_{13.2} = 0$ and $r_{14.23} = 0$, both of which should hold in order for all of the simultaneous equations to be consistent under this causal model. It also turns out that in this particular model we need not control for X_3 in order to have the partial between X_1 and X_4 vanish. This can be seen from the equation

$$r_{14.23} = \frac{r_{14.2} - r_{13.2}r_{34.2}}{\sqrt{1 - r^2_{13.2}}\,\sqrt{1 - r^2_{34.2}}} .$$

Since the model predicts that $r_{13.2}$ and $r_{14.23}$ should both disappear, it immediately follows that $r_{14.2}$ should also be approximately zero, except for sampling error.

In this particular instance, when considering the partial between X_1 and X_4, we need not control for X_3 since both the direct and indirect effects of X_2 on X_4 are contained in r_{24}. To control for the intervening variable X_3 would be redundant, although there is no harm in doing so. There are a number of other four-variable models in which a similar principle operates. In any given case, one can always examine the formula for the higher-order partial to see if a particular lower-order partial also vanishes.

Finally let us remove the arrow between X_2 and X_4, giving us a model in which there is a simple causal chain from X_1 to X_2 to X_3 to X_4, as in Figure 6. According to the general rule there will now be three predictions: $r_{13.2} = 0$, $r_{14.23} = 0$, and $r_{24.13} = 0$. But we find that a number of lower-order partials likewise vanish. In particular, both $r_{14.2}$ and $r_{14.3}$ should be zero, as can easily be verified from the formulas. This means that *in such a simple causal chain one may control for either of the intervening variables and still have the partial between the two end variables vanish*.

In the particular four-variable case of Figure 6 we get the very simple result that

$$r_{14} = r_{12}r_{23}r_{34},$$

indicating that the correlation between the two end variables is weaker numerically than any of the correlations between intermediate variables. This result, which is consistent with common sense, can be readily extended to any number of variables.

It also turns out that for the model represented in Figure 6 we can expect $r_{24.3}$ as well as $r_{24.13}$ to vanish. This illustrates another principle that also appears to hold more generally.[4] *Whenever a variable* (in this case X_1) *operates on only one member of a set of other variables* (here X_2, X_3, and X_4), *we do not need to control for this former variable in order to have the appropriate*

4. *Ibid.*, pp. 191-92.

partials among the other variables disappear. This is in accord with our requirements about outside variables that might possibly operate as disturbing influences. As long as a factor is a causal determinant of only one endogenous variable, we need not be concerned about its disturbing effects.

In the particular model under consideration, X_1 is an antecedent cause that operates only on X_2 and does not disturb the patterning of relationships among the remaining variables. In relating X_2 to X_4, we need only control for the intervening variable in order to have the partial vanish. This does not violate our general rule to the effect that partials should disappear whenever one controls for all antecedent or intervening variables. It merely indicates that one does not need to control for all such variables under particular circumstances. But a control for X_1, here, would not produce misleading results. This is in contrast with what might happen if we were to control for a dependent variable.

A Six-Variable Model. Before introducing some illustrative numerical material, it might be well to discuss briefly a six-variable model in order to see how the method can be applied to more complex situations. Suppose we are given the six-variable model of Figure 7. There are fifteen pairs of variables and seven connecting arrows, meaning that we shall have eight prediction equations for use in evaluating the model. At first glance it might seem absurd to attempt to make use of all such equations or even to attempt to write them down. But we can generally expect a number of simplifications to occur. We may also take

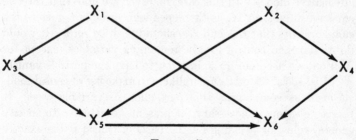

FIGURE 7

advantage of the fact that in examining certain relationships we can ignore any variables that are not prior to or intervening between any of these variables. For example, we can look first at the relationships among X_1, X_2, X_3, and X_4, since none of these variables are caused by X_5 or X_6. In this particular model we note that there are only two arrows connecting these first four variables: X_1 is a cause of X_3, and X_2 is a cause of X_4.

If we can make the required assumptions about outside influences, this means that the four prediction equations for these particular variables reduce to

$$r_{12} = 0 \qquad\qquad r_{14} = 0$$
$$r_{23} = 0 \qquad\qquad r_{34} = 0.$$

In view of these extremely simple predictions, we can also expect some of the remaining equations to simplify. The rule tells us to relate all pairs of unconnected variables and to control for all variables that are not causally dependent on both variables in the pair. This would give the equations

$$r_{15.234} = 0 \qquad\qquad r_{26.1345} = 0$$
$$r_{45.123} = 0 \qquad\qquad r_{36.1245} = 0.$$

Ordinarily it will not be worth one's effort to attempt to ascertain which, if any, of the lower-order partials can also be expected to disappear. The availability of high-speed computers should make it possible to obtain various combinations of higher-order partials, including some which would be inappropriate for this particular model but which might be used to evaluate an alternative model. In this case, however, we note that the two equations involving X_5 as the dependent variable reduce to the simple results that $r_{15.3}$ and $r_{45.2}$ should both be zero. It would do no harm to control for the remaining variables (except for X_6), but we need not do so in order to have the partials vanish.

Most social scientists are unlikely to make use of causal models even as complex as this particular six-variable case. It therefore seems unnecessary, at present, to attempt to specify general rules for deciding on the basis of causal paths exactly which of the lower-order partials should vanish in any particular instance. It is important to realize, however, that the very simple three-variable models commonly discussed in the literature are special cases of more complex models and that in principle we may extend the analysis to include any number of variables. But as we have pointed out previously, *the more such variables we wish to include the more necessary it becomes to confine our attention to simple linear additive models. If we wish to introduce complexities in the form of additional variables brought explicitly into the causal system, we must ordinarily pay the price of oversimplifications of another type.*

NUMERICAL APPLICATIONS

We shall now apply this method for making causal inferences, which for brevity will be referred to as Simon's method, to two very different types of empirical problems. The first involves anthropological data and an attempt to infer evolutionary sequences; the second makes use of census data and is concerned with the prediction of white and nonwhite levels of living. In the first application the method will be used to choose between alternative models which were developed a priori. In the second case we shall discuss how it can be used in exploratory fashion to develop successive models that are progressively more and more consistent with the data.

In the first application it will be seen that the method can be applied to attributes as well as to data that have been measured more precisely in terms of interval scales. Since the measure ϕ can be considered a special case of r in 2×2 tables, we can predict that partial ϕ's will disappear under the same causal conditions as in instances where more precise measurement has been possible.[5] Results must be interpreted much more cautiously however. In part this is owing to the fact that the numerical value of ϕ is dependent on the nature of the marginal totals in a 2×2 table, and these, in turn, depend upon the way the data have been dichotomized.

The fact that cutpoints are often arbitrary in the case of

5. Since the use of crude categories often involves considerable measurement error, this statement is only approximately correct. See Chapter V.

classified data is a general disadvantage of these crude measurement techniques. We shall later have occasion to examine situations in which inferences based on attribute data can be misleading. But if done cautiously, one may still attempt to make causal interpretations of such data. It is an obvious fact that many data can presently be measured only very crudely, and we shall have to learn to handle them as well as possible given these limitations.

North American Indian Data.[6] An important problem for anthropologists and sociologists concerns the issue of whether or not certain evolutionary sequences in the development of culture can be established. Unfortunately, we often lack data on the exact temporal sequences involved. A society may have been studied at a single point in time, or over a relatively short interval, and the only reliable data available may consist of a list of characteristics that are either present or absent at that given time. The question of which traits appeared first, and which were linked directly and which indirectly through the operation of intervening variables, may be lost in history.

In illustrating the use of Simon's method, we shall make use of some data on North American Indian tribes presented by Driver and Massey.[7] In brief, Driver and Massey attempted to assess the relative merits of evolutionary theories of culture by analyzing various intercorrelations among culture traits for 280 North American Indian tribes. Although these authors were also concerned with a fifth variable, kinship terminologies, we may simplify the picture somewhat by confining our attention to four variables: division of labor, postnuptial residence, land tenure, and descent. According to the particular evolutionist theory tested by Driver and Massey, it was argued that a matridominant division of labor (W) should be followed by matrilocal residence (X), then by matricentered land tenure

6. This section represents a slightly revised version of portions of the author's paper, "Correlational Analysis and Causal Inferences," *American Anthropologist*, LXII (August, 1960), 624-31.

7. H. E. Driver and W. C. Massey, *Comparative Studies of North American Indians* (Philadelphia: The American Philosophical Society, 1957), pp. 427-34.

(Y), and finally by a matrilineal system of descent (Z). Thus the causal chain involved can be diagrammed as

$$W \rightarrow X \rightarrow Y \rightarrow Z.$$

The authors reasoned that since at each stage in the process a certain time lag would be involved, making perfect correlations unlikely, we would ordinarily expect the largest correlations to occur between adjacent variables in whatever causal chain were operating. Thus in the above model we would expect the correlation between W and Y to be smaller than those between W and X, on the one hand, and X and Y on the other. The smallest correlations should therefore occur between variables furthest removed from each other in the causal chain (i.e., W and Z). The authors then proceeded to take the arithmetic mean of all correlations between adjacent pairs $(WX, XY,$ and $YZ)$, comparing this mean with the means for pairs removed from one another by a single step $(WY$ and $XZ)$ and with those removed by two steps (in this case only WZ) Under the assumed model, these correlation means should decrease in magnitude as the number of steps between variables is increased. Generally speaking, the data turned out to support this particular causal model.

Making use of Simon's technique, let us examine this simple causal chain, which we shall refer to as Model I. For this particular model we have seen that not only should

$$r_{xz.y} = 0, \ or \ r_{xz} = r_{xy}r_{yz}$$

and

$$r_{wy.x} = 0, \ or \ r_{wy} = r_{wx}r_{xy}$$

but also

$$r_{wz} = r_{wx}r_{xy}r_{yz}.$$

This is, of course, consistent with Driver and Massey's argument that the magnitude of the correlations should be smaller between variables furthest removed from one another in the causal sequence. But we can also predict exactly how large each correlation should be in relation to the others.

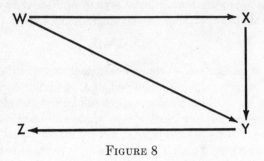

Notice that we need not assume that the pattern among correlations is primarily owing to a time-lag factor. We have a more general formulation in which we admit the operation of variables outside the system of four variables. Some of these other variables not taken into consideration may indeed help to create a time lag. For example, other cultural patterns such as the level of technology, certain sacred beliefs and practices, or the vested interests of various powerful individuals may influence the rate of change, thus partially accounting for the imperfect correlations. We do not have to assume that the correlations would be perfect were it not for a time lag, however.

We can now consider an alternative causal model, appropriate to the same data, suggested by David F. Aberle before his knowledge of the predictions derived by Simon's method. In this model (see Figure 8) we not only have a simple causal chain, but there is also a direct link between the division of labor (W) and land tenure (Y). Applying Simon's technique to this second model, we now can make the following predictions

$$r_{xz} = r_{xy}r_{yz} \quad (\text{since } r_{xz \cdot wy} = r_{xz \cdot y} = 0),$$

and

$$r_{wz} = r_{wy}r_{yz}.$$

Notice that the first of these equations is predicted by Model I. The second can also be derived from Model I *if and only if* $r_{wy} = r_{wx}r_{xy}$. Since Model II does not require this latter equation to hold—and in fact predicts that r_{wy} will be greater than this product if all causal links are positive—we may readily distinguish empirically between the two models.

Making use of the intercorrelations for matridominant traits supplied by Driver and Massey, let us see which of the above two models best fits the data. The values of r ($=\phi$) are given in Table 1. The predictions and degrees of fit for the two models are summarized in Table 2. We see immediately that the second causal model provides the better set of predictions for these particular data. Both the correlations between division of labor and land tenure (r_{wy}), and between division of

Table 1. Intercorrelations for Matricentered Traits of North American Indians.

	W	X	Y	Z
Matridominant Division of Labor (W)	—	.49	.53	.39
Matrilocal Residence (X)	.49	—	.61	.51
Matricentered Land Tenure (Y)	.53	.61	—	.80
Matrilineal Descent (Z)	.39	.51	.80	—

Source: H. E. Driver and W. C. Massey, *Comparative Studies of North American Indians* (Philadelphia: The American Philosophical Society, 1957), p. 432.

Table 2. Predictions and Degrees of Fit of Models I and II for Matricentered Traits of North American Indians.

*Predictions**	*Degrees of Fit*
	Model I
	Actual Expected
$r_{zz}=r_{xy}r_{yz}$	.51 *vs.* .49 = (.61) (.80)
$r_{wy}=r_{wx}r_{xy}$	.53 *vs.* .30 = (.49) (.61)
$r_{wz}=r_{wx}r_{xy}r_{yz}$	.39 *vs.* .24 = (.49) (.61) (.80)
	Model II
$r_{zz}=r_{xy}r_{yz}$	.51 *vs.* .49 = (.61) (.80)
$r_{wz}=r_{wy}r_{yz}$	.39 *vs.* .42 = (.53) (.80)

*These predictions could also be stated, alternatively, in terms of the disappearance of the appropriate partials.

labor and descent (r_{wz}), are numerically larger than would be predicted by a simple causal chain.   In Model II, by adding an arrow directly linking the division of labor with land tenure, we essentially shorten the linkage between division of labor and descent, thereby raising the magnitude of r_{wz} since all correlations are positive.

It should be explicitly noted that we have *not* established the validity of Model II.   We have merely eliminated Model I. As pointed out previously, there will ordinarily be several models that yield identical predictions.   In particular, we cannot distinguish between Model I and the situation in which all arrows have been reversed, i.e., $Z{\rightarrow}Y{\rightarrow}X{\rightarrow}W$.   But one cannot generally reverse all arrows and come up with a model giving the same predictions, although Model II above is another exception. *When we get beyond the simple three-variable case, there will of course be a very large number of possible alternatives, only a relatively small number of which will give exactly the same sets of predictions. Usually, therefore, one will find it possible to distinguish between any two models that appear to be realistic theoretical alternatives.*

It is sometimes possible to distinguish between two models that give the same predictions by adding another variable.   For example, had the data turned out to be consistent with Model I, and had our attention been originally focused on the three variables X, Y, and Z, we would not have been able to distinguish between $X{\rightarrow}Y{\rightarrow}Z$ and $X{\leftarrow}Y{\rightarrow}Z$.   Both models predict that $r_{xz \cdot y} = 0$.   But if we could assume that W caused X but not Y we could, by adding W, decide between the two.   In the first case we would have the model $W{\rightarrow}X{\rightarrow}Y{\rightarrow}Z$, giving the prediction that $r_{wy} = r_{wx}r_{xy}$.   But the second alternative gives $W{\rightarrow}X{\leftarrow}Y{\rightarrow}Z$, which implies that r_{wy} should be approximately zero.

Such a procedure of adding another variable is of course not completely empirical.   It depends upon certain assumptions about the causal relationships between W and the other variables.   These assumptions can sometimes be subjected to empirical test, however.   We have seen that the Driver and Massey

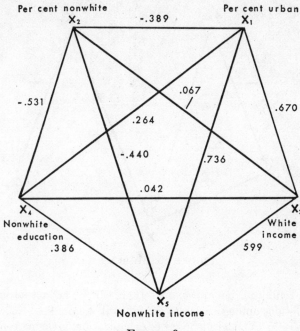

Per cent nonwhite
X_2 -.389   Per cent urban
X_1

-.531   .067   .670

.264

-.440   .736

.042

X_4 X_3
Nonwhite   White
education   income
.386   599

X_5
Nonwhite income

FIGURE 9

data are more consistent with Model II in which W is a cause of Y as well as of X. As can easily be shown, if W is also a cause of Y, we cannot use W in this simple manner to infer the direction of the causal arrow between X and Y.

Census Data on Discrimination.[8]   The second set of data we shall use were taken from the 1950 census, the units of analysis being 150 randomly selected Southern counties. A sample of size 150 is perhaps somewhat too small to permit one to ignore sampling error, but since our purpose is to illustrate a methodological technique rather than to discuss substantive issues, the problem of sampling error will be ignored. All relationships

8. This section represents a slightly revised version of portions of the author's paper, "Correlation and Causality: the Multivariate Case," *Social Forces* XXXIX (March, 1961), 246-51.

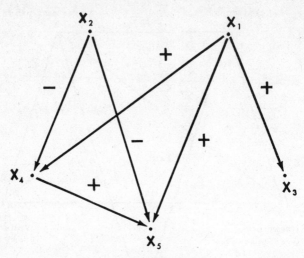

FIGURE 10. MODEL I

were found to be approximately linear. The actual inter-correlations among variables are given in Figure 9.

Variable X_1, a crude index of urbanization, is the percentage of the county's population classed as either urban or rural nonfarm. X_2 represents the percentage of nonwhites in the county. Variables X_3 and X_5 involve measures of white and nonwhite incomes, respectively (the percentage of families with annual income of \$1,500 or more), and X_4 is an index of nonwhite educational levels (percentage of males twenty-five and over with more than six years of schooling).

(a) *Model I*. The first exploratory causal model is given in Figure 10. Notice that the urbanization index (X_1) and per cent nonwhite (X_2) have been conceived as independent causes of nonwhite educational and income levels. X_1 is also presumed to cause changes in white incomes, the relationship between white and nonwhite incomes being spurious. In other words, both white and nonwhite incomes are expected to rise and fall according to economic conditions, without the one directly affecting the other. Finally, nonwhite education is assumed to affect nonwhite incomes, though the relationship between these two variables is also partly spurious (owing to X_1 and X_2).

We need not assume that per cent nonwhite, per se, is a direct determinant, in some absolute sense, of nonwhite income and educational levels. Presumably, an increase in the minority percentage affects such factors as the degree of competition with the minority, the political threat by the minority, or gains from minority exploitation. But none of these latter intervening variables have been brought into the theoretical system, and, therefore, we can conceive of the relationships between X_2 and X_4 and between X_2 and X_5 as being "direct." Essentially the same argument would apply to each of the remaining causal arrows.

The prediction equations for Model I are given in the top set of rows of Table 3. Since there are six arrows and ten pairs of

Table 3. Predictions and Degrees of Fit for Models I, II, and III

	Predictions		*Degrees of Fit*	
		Model I		
			Actual	Expected
$r_{12}=0$			$-.39$ *vs.*	0
$r_{23}=0$			$.07$ *vs.*	0
$r_{34}=r_{13}r_{14}$			$.04$ *vs.*	$.18=(.670)(.264)$
$r_{35}=r_{13}r_{15}$			$.60$ *vs.*	$.49=(.670)(.736)$
		Model II		
$r_{23}=r_{12}r_{13}$			$.07$ *vs.*	$-.26=(-.389)(.670)$
$r_{34}=r_{13}r_{14}$			$.04$ *vs.*	$.18=(.670)(.264)$
$r_{35}=r_{13}r_{15}$			$.60$ *vs.*	$.49=(.670)(.736)$
		Model III		
$r_{14}=r_{12}r_{24}$			$.26$ *vs.*	$.21=(-.389)(-.531)$
$r_{34}=r_{23}r_{24}$			$.04$ *vs.*	$-.04=(.067)(-.531)$
$r_{35}=r_{13}r_{15}+\dfrac{(r_{23}-r_{12}r_{13})(r_{25}-r_{12}r_{15})}{1-r^2_{12}}$			$.60$ *vs.*	$.43=.49+(-.06)$

variables there are four predictions, one for each of the unconnected variables. Notice that three of the four predictions are reasonably good, but the first is quite poor. It is not easy to develop an entirely satisfactory set of criteria for evaluating the adequacy of the goodness of fit. But we can proceed in ex-post-facto manner to look for models that are at least theoretically plausible and that will yield somewhat better predictions. These latter models can then be actually tested on another set of data.

We shall need some rules of thumb for modifying the causal model since the addition (or subtraction) of a single arrow may make several changes in the prediction equations. Two such rules are as follows: (1) *make changes where there are the largest discrepancies between actual and predicted values; and* (2) *where possible, make changes first in causal relationships among variables presumed to be operating near the beginning of the causal sequence,* i.e. those variables that are taken to be the most independent of the others. Here both criteria point to the relationship between X_1 and X_2: not only does r_{12} differ considerably from the predicted value of zero, but these two variables have been taken as independent of the other three.

The data immediately suggest adding an arrow between X_1 and X_2, unless we wish to introduce a sixth variable into the system. Historically, of course, we know that Negro slaves were imported because of the South's plantation economy and that nonwhites have tended to remain in rural areas until only very recently. Although it would be possible to argue that it was the presence of a high percentage of nonwhites which has caused certain counties to remain rural, or which has delayed their urbanization, we shall draw the arrow from X_1 to X_2. (See Model II, Figure 11.) As in many other empirical instances, we seem to have a case of two-way causation, but with the strength of the causal relationship being perhaps more pronounced in one direction than in the other. One of the most valuable by-products of Simon's approach may well be the pinpointing of such specific causal issues. In any instances where a major theoretical problem is raised, several alternative models can be developed in order to see which proposed causal ordering gives the better predictions.

(b) *Model II.* Model II is presented in Figure 11, and predictions from this model are also found in Table 3. Notice

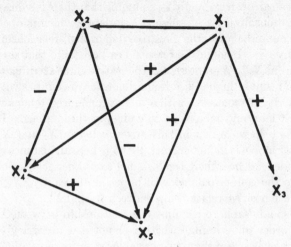

FIGURE 11. MODEL II

that the addition of an arrow from X_1 to X_2 does not affect the predictions for r_{34} and r_{35}, although it will often be the case that adding or subtracting an arrow between two variables will change predicted relationships among variables other than the two directly involved.

We now have a poorer prediction for r_{23}, however. By directly linking X_1 and X_2 we imply that there should be a correlation between X_2 and X_3, albeit a spurious relationship. Since X_1 is related oppositely to X_2 and X_3, the value of r_{23} should be negative, whereas actually it is slightly positive. Model II predicts that urban counties should have both high white incomes and low minority percentages. Therefore counties having high white incomes (predominantly urban) should have low percentages of nonwhites, but a control for X_1 should produce a zero partial correlation between X_2 and X_3. Actually, the partial is .48.

In order to develop a better-fitting model, we could introduce additional variables that would account for such a discrepancy. Or we could confine ourselves to the original five variables, drawing in an arrow from X_2 to X_3, assuming that there is a direct *positive* relationship between these two variables which is operating to counterbalance the negative (spurious) relationship produced by X_1. It might be reasoned ex post facto that such an arrow from X_2 to X_3 represents exploitative gains accruing to whites as a result of higher discrimination rates in counties with larger minority percentages, with a more pronounced tendency for the best land and jobs to go to whites in these areas. In Model III we have drawn in this arrow between X_2 and X_3. If this latter model is in fact correct, we have here an instance of spurious independence where the lack of a zero-order correlation is owing to the counterbalancing of opposing forces, i.e., X_1 is obscuring the positive relationship between X_2 and X_3.

It is also advisable to examine the relationship between X_1 and X_4 in order to determine whether or not it is necessary to keep the arrow between these two variables after we have added the arrow connecting X_1 and X_2. A purely theoretical case can be made for retaining it by simply assuming that urbanization, per se, produces better educational opportunities for nonwhites. But suppose we were to erase this arrow. It can easily be shown that the prediction equation $r_{14} = r_{12}r_{24}$ would result (see predictions for Model III). Numerically we get .26 versus .21, a reasonably close prediction.

The relatively low numerical value of r_{14} therefore indicates that we do not need to assume a direct as well as an indirect relationship between X_1 and X_4. For illustrative purposes we shall drop the arrow between X_1 and X_4, though in so doing we again raise some interesting theoretical questions. If data were available, we might look for an outside disturbing influence, such as selective migration, which could be operating to reduce the magnitude of r_{14}.

(c) *Model III*. The third model (see Figure 12 and Table 3) can be considered more briefly. We have made the two changes mentioned above: there is now an arrow from X_2 to X_3 but none between X_1 and X_4. The latter change introduces the prediction equation for r_{14} which we have already discussed. The new equation for r_{34} also gives a somewhat better prediction

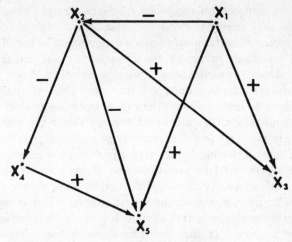

FIGURE 12. MODEL III

than previously, though such a gain may well be due to sampling errors.

The prediction for r_{35} is now less satisfactory, however, because of the correction factor added to the $r_{13}r_{15}$ term. Note the effect of the arrow between X_2 and X_3. Ignoring the effects of X_1, we see that X_2 works to produce a negative (spurious) correlation between X_3 and X_5. This essentially cancels a portion of the positive relationship between X_3 and X_5 due to X_1, reducing the expected value to .43 as compared with the actual value of .60. Thus the actual correlation between white and nonwhite incomes is higher than that predicted by Model III. This suggests either drawing in a direct arrow or introducing an additional variable. We may also consider the predicted relationship between X_4 and X_5 if the direct arrow were erased. The expected value of r_{45} $(= .39)$ would be $r_{24}r_{25}$ $(= .23)$, and we would again be faced with a similar decision.

SOME CAUTIONS

Spuriousness Versus Alternative Models. When one's focus is directly on forms of relationships, it is obvious that concern should be centered on regression coefficients rather than correlations that merely measure goodness of fit. But in testing the adequacy of certain causal models we may make use of prediction equations involving the disappearance of either the partial slopes or correlations. Since correlations have relatively simple interpretations and an upper limit of unity, it would seem to make more sense in these instances to deal with correlations rather than slopes. Certainly this is the common practice in sociology as well as psychology and social psychology.

We have been considering certain pure or ideal cases where we can expect partial correlations and slopes actually to disappear. Heuristically, it is useful to study these simple cases in order to provide a rationale for controlling. But in actual research we may rarely find that such partials are completely reduced to zero. It may be difficult to distinguish among several alternative models because of the influence of measurement errors or confounding influences. Under circumstances where partials do not reduce to zero, we may find that partial correlations and slopes do not behave similarly, and we must be particularly on guard against making faulty inferences.

One of the most common sorts of models tested in empirical research is one in which we postulate that the relationship between X and Y is spurious owing to one or more common causes. In view of the fact that in the exploratory stages of any science one of the most important tasks is to eliminate numerous possible explanatory variables, such tests for spuriousness are highly necessary and very appropriate in any piece of research.

Perhaps the main pitfall to be avoided in inferring spurious relationships is the possibility of confusing this particular kind of model with others that predict the same or similar empirical results. In the simple three-variable case, the models $X \leftarrow Z \rightarrow Y$ and $X \rightarrow Z \rightarrow Y$ yield the same empirical prediction that $r_{xy \cdot z} = 0$. In the first model the relationship between X and Y is spurious. But in the second model X is an indirect cause of Y through Z, and we would not ordinarily attempt to control for Z in an experimental situation. In such an instance, Z is referred to as providing an "interpretation" of the relationship between X and Y. One might see no theoretical reason why there should be a direct causal link between the two variables. He then searches for an intervening variable that, when controlled, makes the original correlation between X and Y disappear. If it does so, presumably he has been able to interpret the relationship, or to understand more clearly the links involved.

In a very real sense, through interpretation one is putting frosting on the cake, so to speak. He is not discovering anything radically wrong with the notion that X causes Y. He is merely making it seem more plausible by finding the intermediate links. Obviously there is theoretically no end to the interpretive process, as one can practically always take any two variables that are causally related and insert intervening variables, thereby converting what was originally conceived to be a direct relationship into an indirect one. Such an interpretive process would seem to be particularly useful during the more advanced stages of a science, when one is attempting to spell out the finer points of a theory. Another use for interpretation consists of looking for possible interaction and in specifying the conditions under which a given relationship either does or does not hold. For example, one might find that X is an indirect cause of Y only when Z intervenes in a certain way.[9]

There are other alternative models that do not yield exactly the same predictions as in the case of spuriousness but that can easily be confused with the spurious model in practice. An important case is one where we are dealing with a developmental sequence of the form $W \rightarrow X \rightarrow Y$. A control for W will ordinarily reduce the magnitude of r_{xy}, though it will not affect the expected value of b_{yx}. This can be shown by substituting the prediction $r_{wy} = r_{wx}r_{xy}$ into the formulas for $r_{xy \cdot w}$ and $b_{yx \cdot w}$.

The relative reduction in the correlation coefficient depends on the strength of the relationship between W and X. The

9. For excellent discussions of the interpretive process, see Herbert Hyman, *Survey Designs and Analysis* (Glencoe: The Free Press, 1955), Chapter 7; and Paul Lazarsfeld, "Interpretation of Statistical Relationships as a Research Operation," in P. Lazarsfeld and M. Rosenberg (eds.), *The Language of Social Research* (Glencoe: The Free Press, 1955), pp. 115-25.

stronger this correlation, the greater the size of the reduction. In common-sense terms, we would expect that a control for a major cause of X will substantially reduce the variation in X, thereby diminishing the proportion of the variation in Y that will be explained by X. But the nature of the causal law relating X and Y should be unaffected by a control for W under the assumed model.

One is especially likely to confuse developmental sequences with spurious relationships in dealing with so-called "background variables" (e.g., age, sex, and race), which serve as imperfect indicators of other variables.[10] Because of the measurement errors involved, if we control for the background factor, we do not expect the partial correlation to vanish even if the relationship is completely spurious.[11] The correlation will merely be reduced in magnitude. But how can we then distinguish a case of spuriousness from one involving a developmental sequence? In both cases we may assume the background variable to be a cause of X, either directly or indirectly. The crucial question, however, is whether or not this variable is also a cause of Y other than through X. If so, then the relationship between X and Y may be at least partly spurious. Or we may be dealing with a more complex model where X causes Y but where the background variable creates a confounding influence by also operating directly on Y.

Here the focus of attention should be on the nature of the causal law and regression coefficients, rather than on partial correlations. In the "pure" developmental sequence $W \rightarrow X \rightarrow Y$, we should not be controlling for the antecedent cause W in relating X to Y. If we happen to do so by mistake the expected value of b_{yx} will be unaffected, as is appropriate. But if the correct model happens to be $X \leftarrow W \rightarrow Y$, *both* the partial correlation and partial slope will be reduced to zero. *In other words, if we focus on the slope we make the correct inference in*

10. See Hyman, *Survey Design and Analysis*, pp. 254-63.

11. As will be discussed in Chapter V, random measurement error in W for either of the models $X \leftarrow W \rightarrow Y$ or $X \rightarrow W \rightarrow Y$ will result in the failure of $r_{xy \cdot w}$ to reduce completely to zero.

*either case. In instances where a control for W reduces the corre-
lation between X and Y but leaves the slope unchanged, we would be
on safer grounds in inferring a developmental sequence rather than
a spurious relationship. The mere fact that a partial correlation
goes down is not enough to infer spuriousness.*

As a general rule, we might rather dogmatically assert that
whenever one's attention is to be focused on the nature of causal
laws, he will be on safer grounds comparing the behavior of regression coefficients rather than correlation coefficients. An
exception to this rule can be made in instances where a correlation coefficient is actually expected to vanish. But this exception does not include instances where a partial is merely *reduced* in
magnitude. The numerical value of a correlation coefficient
may be reduced not only because a confounding influence has
been controlled, but it may also be altered because we have decreased the total variation in the independent variable relative
to that in other causes of the dependent variable. This particular point will again be emphasized in the following chapter.

Sampling Error and Multicollinearity. If multivariate normality in the population could be assumed, one might make a
series of significance tests to determine departures from chance
under the null hypothesis that a given population partial correlation (or slope) is zero. Better still, one might construct
confidence intervals about each of the coefficients since he
should be primarily interested in the magnitude of the departures from zero.

The problem of evaluating sampling error is especially
complicated whenever we must deal with simultaneous equations. As pointed out previously, simple recursive systems have
very real advantages over more general structural equations
whose coefficients cannot be adequately estimated by ordinary
least squares. At the present stage in the development of most
social sciences, it is probably not necessary to become involved
with the complex problems of identifiability and various alternative procedures for obtaining estimates of the coefficients in
structural systems.[12] It will suffice to point up one type of

12. For a discussion of alternative estimating procedures, see J. Johnston,

difficulty involving sampling error which seems to arise fairly frequently in sociological and psychological studies. This is the problem of multicollinearity where two or more supposedly "independent" variables are highly correlated.

Suppose we wish to explain the variation in some dependent variable Y in terms of two other variables X and Z, which are highly correlated. The reasons for this initial correlation may be unknown or not easily subjected to empirical test. X may cause Z, or vice versa. Or their correlation may be owing to some additional variables that are producing a spurious relationship. Regardless of the reasons for this correlation, its net effect is to increase the sampling errors of both $r_{xy \cdot z}$ and $r_{zy \cdot x}$. In the limiting case where X and Z are perfectly correlated, these sampling errors become infinite.[13]

The reason why sampling errors become infinite when X and Z are perfectly related is that we can form arbitrary linear combinations of the two simultaneous equations, making the regression coefficients indeterminate. Consider the equation

$$Y = 2 + 5X - 3Z + e$$

If X and Z are perfectly related, say by the equation

$$Z = 2 + 3X$$

then we can multiply the second equation by any constant and add it to the first. For example, multiplying by two we would get

$$0 = 4 + 6X - 2Z$$

which when added to the first equation would give

$$Y = 6 + 11X - 5Z + e.$$

This new equation is mathematically equivalent to the original one, though the coefficients differ. Clearly, there are

Econometric Methods (New York: McGraw-Hill Book Company, 1963), Chapter 9.

13. Wold and Jureen, *Demand Analysis*, pp. 46-48. See also Johnston, *Econometric Methods*, pp. 201-7, and H. M. Blalock, "Correlated Independent Variables: The Problem of Multicollinearity," *Social Forces*, XLII (December, 1963), 233-37.

an indefinite number of such sets of coefficients, including sets in which the coefficient of either X or Z will be zero. The same indeterminate results will also occur in the case of partial correlation coefficients.

Whenever the relationship between X and Z is imperfect, we will find unique least-squares solutions, but the stronger the correlation between X and Z the more solutions that will fit the data almost equally well. In practical terms, this means that with slight changes owing to sampling (or measurement) error, the partial slopes and correlations may be altered considerably. For example, suppose r_{xz} is .80, the values of r_{xy} and r_{yz} being .60 and .50 respectively. Then $r_{xy \cdot z}$ is equal to .38 numerically. But if the magnitudes of the latter two correlations were reversed, as might very well happen as a result of sampling fluctuations, the partial would take on the value of .04. In the second instance we might be led to infer a spurious relationship between X and Y, whereas in the first we would not.

A high correlation between the two independent variables, by giving rise to considerable sampling error, therefore makes it difficult to choose reliably between alternative models. In experimental designs one deliberately attempts to manipulate the several independent variables in such a way that their effects on the dependent variable are completely unrelated and can be easily isolated. He can then readily attribute a certain portion of the variation to each of the independent variables in turn. But when these latter variables are highly associated, their relative effects become difficult to disentangle unless both measurement and sampling errors can be considerably reduced. The problem of evaluating their relative importance or the adequacy of any particular causal model then becomes a risky business.

One possible way out of the difficulty posed by multicollinearity is to make two independent variables completely unrelated in a *sample*, even though they are highly correlated in the population. This can readily be achieved through stratification, which has a certain analogy with manipulations in experimental designs. For example, suppose we are interested in trying to separate out the effects of race and occupation on a particular attitude or voting behavior. Ordinarily, race and occupation will be highly related, with there being relatively few Negroes in white-collar occupations. But through stratification we might select, say, 50 males in each of the following categories: Negro white-collar, Negro blue-collar, white white-collar, and white blue-collar. Because of the crudity of such a dichotomization of occupations, this would undoubtedly not make the two variables completely unrelated, since Negro white-collar occupants are likely to have somewhat lower-level occupations than their white counterparts. But in the sample we would have the two variables almost unrelated to each other. Could we then proceed to analyze their separate effects?

In the ideal experimental design we can supposedly assume that disturbing influences operate only *after* individuals have been assigned to experimental and control groups. Effects of previous influences are hopefully canceled through randomization. But in sample surveys no such simple assumptions can reasonably be made. For example, there undoubtedly are a number of variables that determine occupation in addition to one's race. Native intelligence and ambition are two such factors. In taking equal numbers of cases in each of the four subtypes, we are in effect oversampling the Negro white-collar and white blue-collar populations. Thus we are apt, also, to oversample Negroes with high ambition and ability. Put another way, if we are given a group of whites and Negroes with similar occupations, we expect the Negro sample to contain relatively more individuals with higher ability and ambition. The effects of these latter variables then become confounded with those of race. The gains in making race and occupation unrelated in the sample may be only apparent.

Therefore, in manipulating one's sample design so as to take out the multicollinearity effect, one may inadvertently introduce confounding influences. In the above example as long as ability and ambition have no direct effects on the dependent variable (e.g., an attitude or voting behavior), one may still find it possible to make correct inferences regarding the separate effects of race and occupation. But what if they do affect the dependent variable? Preliminary results with artificial data seem to indicate that complications may be serious. Considerably more research on the subject needs to be carried out, however, before definitive answers can be given.

Nonadditive Models. We have been forced to assume both linear relationships and additive effects of independent variables. Fortunately, both of these assumptions can be tested empirically, and often one can find relatively simple transformations that will make these particular restrictive assumptions sufficiently realistic. The problems of specification and interaction have been discussed at length in the research methods literature and need not be dealt with in detail in the present connection.[14] Our main purpose is merely to alert the reader to their possibility.

In instances where interaction is found, ordinary language seems most inadequate for describing the relationships involved. It is very simple to say, "If X increases Y increases at a constant rate, other things being equal." But interaction requires a more complex statement of the form, "As Z changes, the *relationship* between X and Y changes in a given manner." Several such statements, when put together, not only become clumsy on the verbal level, but it is much more difficult to trace out their logical implications. The use of mathematical models would therefore seem especially appropriate where an interaction effect has been found.

To illustrate the use of mathematical models in instances where interaction occurs, we can briefly discuss two types of nonadditive situations. Suppose one finds that when Z is low there is virtually no relationship between X and Y. But as Z increases, the relationship between X and Y may become stronger and stronger. In such a case the slope of the relationship between X and Y is also likely to increase with Z rather than to remain constant. A multiplicative model of the form $Y = kXZ$ would immediately be suggested.

One might also allow for a nonlinear relationship between X and Y, for fixed values of Z, by using the equation $Y = kX^bZ^c$,

14. See especially Hyman, *Survey Design and Analysis*, Chapter 7.

where the coefficients b and c could take on any values, positive or negative. For example, a negative value of c would indicate that X^b is to be divided by Z raised to a positive power. If such multiplicative models could be postulated, then simple logarithmic transformations could be used to turn the relationship into a linear additive one, as is commonly done with supply and demand functions in economics. We could thus write

$$\log Y = \log k + b(\log X) + c(\log Z)$$

and then make use of standard least-squares procedures.

Multiplicative relationships of this form may not be too uncommon in sociology and psychology, but they may go relatively unnoticed when one is dealing primarily with qualitative data and where the analysis stops with a mere specification of conditions rather than an attempt to fit all variables together in a more complex equation. Such models have been used in motivation theories in which the strength of motivation has been taken as a multiplicative function of some internal state (e.g., strength of drive, goal, or motive) and the value of the incentive (e.g., amount of food).[15] A multiplicative model, as contrasted with an additive one, would in this case predict that a large food reward would produce a steeper slope between degree of hunger and intensity of effort to reach the food than would a smaller amount of food.

Lenski's work with status crystallization also illustrates a case of an interaction effect.[16] Although a variable such as political conservatism may increase with both education and income, the essence of Lenski's findings is that there may be an additional effect owing to the size of the *difference* or inconsistency between one's education and income. Other things

15. See John W. Atkinson, "Motivational Determinants of Risk-Taking Behavior," *Psychological Review*, LXIV (November, 1957), pp. 359-72. Actually, Atkinson takes motivation as a multiplicative function of three variables, motive, expectancy, and incentive.

16. See Gerhard E. Lenski, "Status Crystallization: A Non-Vertical Dimension of Social Status," *American Sociological Review*, XIX (August, 1954), 405-13. Lenski's analysis also involved two other dimensions of status, namely occupation and ethnicity.

being equal, the larger such a difference the less conservative the individual. Lenski chooses to introduce another variable, "status crystallization" or "status consistency," into the system. But clearly, the entire relationship can be conceived in terms of three variables (conservatism, education, and income) *if* one makes use of a model that allows for an interaction effect.

For example, one possible model might be as follows:

$$Y = a + b_1 X + b_2 Z - b_3 (X - kZ)^2$$

where the b's are all positive constants. This equation says that conservatism Y increases (linearly) with education X and income Z but that it decreases with the (square of the) difference between education and income. Notice that the introduction of a squared difference term indicates that we are expecting a decrease in conservatism with an increasing differential regardless of the direction of this difference. In other words, the model assumes no basic distinction between high income and low education types, on the one hand, and low income and high education types on the other. This model could then be transformed into an additive one by letting W, a measure of status inconsistency, equal $(X - kZ)^2$.

CONCLUDING REMARKS

In attempting to make causal inferences with actual empirical data, we begin to see not only the advantages of a systematic method such as Simon's but also its limitations and the kinds of complications that may arise. The number of simplifying assumptions that must be made would seem to place very real restrictions on the applicability of the procedure. Some additional complications will be discussed in Chapter V. We have been presuming negligible measurement errors. Some of the variables of theoretical concern may not be directly measured but merely represented by indicators. There may also be outside or exogenous variables which operate as confounding influences, so that the assumptions concerning the behavior of error terms are unrealistic.

We have also not allowed for the possibility that a number

of variables may have been measured in terms of ordinal scales or classified into more than two categories. In such instances, there does not seem to be any really adequate rationale for making causal inferences on the basis of correlational data. In the absence of such a rationale we might tentatively suggest that the same rules for controlling and interpretations for partials be applied, but with proper caution. As we shall see in the next chapter, important information about the amount of variation in each variable may be lost whenever one must resort either to categorized or to ranked data.

While it is true that the use of Pearsonian correlations and regression coefficients is not strictly legitimate unless one has at least an interval scale, it may turn out that it is no more misleading to make use of dubious assumptions about level of measurement than it is to make use of data involving arbitrary cutpoints or ordinal scales that obscure differences in amount of variation. For exploratory purposes it may not be entirely unwise to make use of the rationale developed in connection with higher levels of measurement, even where actual measurement cannot be nearly so precise. This particular point is a matter of conjecture, however, on the basis of present limited research.

Because of these various limitations, we should perhaps look upon the present discussion as indicating the kinds of quantitative methods that might be most appropriate once the social sciences have reached a more advanced stage. Such methods might best be used in a highly exploratory manner, with the recognition that the required assumptions are being only very imperfectly met. We would argue, however, that it is well to have some such methodological tool in mind as an ideal. Otherwise, we may continue to use more or less intuitive methods that do not provide a very clear understanding of exactly what we are doing. Needless to say, considerably more methodological research needs to be carried out before we can adequately understand both the implications and limitations of more systematic techniques.

IV

Inferences Based on Changes in Nonexperimental Designs

A number of practical situations often occur in which, even where adequate data are available, one gets results that appear quite different according to the nature of the study design. Such situations then lead to problems of interpretation which are sometimes quite complex and seemingly paradoxical. The question of ecological correlation is an example of this type of situation. As is well known, one may get different results when dealing with persons as units of analysis from those that would be obtained with census tracts or larger units. The problem posed by ecological correlation can be stated in more general causal terms, however, and the purpose of the present chapter is to examine this more general problem by discussing the behavior of correlation and regression coefficients as they are affected by changes in research design.

In experimental situations we manipulate the independent and control variables and then observe whatever may happen to the dependent variable. We do not directly manipulate the dependent variable itself. In nonexperimental studies the nature of our "manipulations" is quite different. Usually they involve either an initial selection of cases or certain statistical operations on the data after the variables have already been measured.   For example, one may deliberately overweight his extreme cases by giving them a higher probability of appearing in his sample.   Or he may control for a given variable.

Such artificial manipulations, however, admit of a much greater degree of flexibility than is possible in experimental studies.   One can inadvertently manipulate the dependent variable just as easily as the independent variable.   In so doing he may obtain results that can be highly misleading if he wishes to make causal inferences.   Interpretations are not likely to make sense unless these manipulations of numerical data are restricted so as to be permitted only when they have counterparts in the experimental situation.   In particular, manipulations should not be made in terms of the variable or variables that are taken to be dependent.

Our purpose is to examine the behavior of correlation and regression coefficients in comparative situations in which there are varying degrees of control over outside variables.   We shall see that whereas correlation coefficients can be expected to vary, the estimate of the regression coefficient b_{yx} should remain constant, subject to sampling errors.   But this will be true only when manipulations involve the independent variable(s) rather than the dependent variable.   In nonexperimental situations we encounter an important type of problem, one that does not exist to anywhere near the same degree in experimental studies. Basically, this problem involves our inability to find a really effective means for determining direction of causality.

As implied in the opening paragraph, the issue seems to be quite general in nature, but we can conveniently focus on three specific types of instances in which it seems to apply most frequently in social research: (1) where there has been a shift in the units of analysis, (2) where we wish to compare several groups or categories involving the same units of analysis but where the amount of variation in either the dependent or independent variable is itself a variable, and (3) where we are comparing change data with data collected at a single point in time.

CHANGES IN UNITS OF ANALYSIS

The first of these problem areas, involving a change in units, has received considerable attention in the literature.[1] Our own formulation will be somewhat different from, though not inconsistent with, those of other writers. I shall discuss the issue in terms of causal models. In doing so I hope to point out the basic similarities among all three types of comparisons mentioned above.

Robinson's paper on so-called ecological correlations explicitly called attention to a problem that is by no means unique to sociology.[2] Briefly, Robinson argued that it may be incorrect to make inferences about correlations between variables, taking persons as units, on the basis of correlational data based on groups as units. For example, if we correlate delinquency and divorce *rates* for census tracts, we may obtain a relatively high positive correlation. But this does not necessarily mean that individual delinquents come from broken homes. Conceivably, it may even be true that children of divorced parents tend to be nondelinquent. The high delinquency rates in areas of high divorce may be owing to children coming from the relatively smaller number of stable homes. If we were to compare individuals in a 2×2 table, we might find a zero or very weak relationship, whereas correlations based on census tracts might be quite high. Duncan, Cuzzort, and Duncan point out that exactly the same sort of problem arises whenever we shift to units of other types.[3] For example, we might change from

1. See W. S. Robinson, "Ecological Correlations and the Behavior of Individuals," *American Sociological Review*, XV (June, 1950), 351-57; L. A. Goodman, "Ecological Regression and Behavior of Individuals," *American Sociological Review*, XVIII (December, 1953), 663-64; L. A. Goodman, "Some Alternatives to Ecological Correlation," *American Journal of Sociology*, LXIV (May, 1959), 610-25; O. D. Duncan and B. Davis, "An Alternative to Ecological Correlation," *American Sociological Review*, XVIII (December, 1953), 665-66; and O. D. Duncan, R. P. Cuzzort, and B. Duncan, *Statistical Geography* (Glencoe: The Free Press, 1961).

2. Robinson, "Ecological Correlations," *Am. Soc. Rev.*, pp. 351-57.

3. Duncan, Cuzzort, and Duncan, *Statistical Geography*, pp. 9-10. This point was also analyzed in detail in the 1959 paper by Goodman cited in footnote 1.

counties to states as units, or from subregions to whole societies. The shift need not be from one distinct type of unit (e.g., persons) to a completely different type (e.g., groups).

Several writers have indicated that Robinson appears to have overstated the case and that it is in fact possible to make inferences from the one level to the other, provided we are willing to make certain simplifying assumptions.[4]   In particular, we may establish certain boundaries for the correlations on one level if the data are given only on another level. Likewise, we may estimate the values of correlations on a different level, given assumptions of certain kinds. Goodman, especially, has focused on the mathematical relationships between measures on two levels. There is no need to discuss these mathematical properties, since the problem is quite technical and since it has already been summarized elsewhere.[5]

But one can raise the question of how we might translate formal mathematical properties, such as those discussed by Goodman, into the languages of theory and research involving causal models and experimental designs.   In so doing, we shall see the problem in a different perspective that is at least in one respect more general. Put briefly, we shall argue that *in shifting from one unit of analysis to another we are very likely to affect the manner in which outside and possibly disturbing influences are operating on the dependent and independent variables under consideration.*

Philosophically and theoretically, it would be highly upsetting if we were to assume that the fundamental nature of the relationship between two variables changes with every change in units.   For example, if we were to find a particular relationship between some indicator of "anomie" and suicide rates with states as the units of analysis, but a very different one using counties as units, we would be posed with a seemingly signif-

4. See especially the papers by Goodman cited in footnote 1.   In his 1953 paper, the notion of ecological correlation was explicitly replaced by that of regression.   This is essentially similar to the point of view taken in the present chapter.

5. Duncan, Cuzzort, and Duncan, *Statistical Geography*, pp. 60-80.

icant theoretical problem.[6] We would also be unhappy theoretically if one could claim that a redefinition of the states, say into 75 units instead of 50, would markedly change the nature of the relationship between the two variables, as theoretically conceived.

The key to the problem may come with the realization that in shifting units we may be affecting the degree to which *other* unknown or unmeasured variables are influencing the picture. The basic nature of the relationship between anomie and suicides may be the same in counties and states, but in using the larger unit we may in effect be controlling for certain types of disturbing influences. We recognize, for example, that suicides may be caused by all sorts of variables that, from the standpoint of the social scientist, may be taken as "idiosyncratic." One individual may be saved from suicide by an unusually understanding wife or policeman, another by the failure of some mechanical device. If the unit of analysis is relatively small (say a small county or city), the number of suicides may vary considerably from one year to the next. But with a larger unit, such idiosyncratic factors are more likely to cancel each other out, giving a more stable rate. *On mere probability grounds, then, larger units may be much more alike on suicide rates, completely apart from any inherent effects of size, per se, on suicide rates.*[7]

Let us recall Kish's distinction between causes of the dependent variable which are unrelated to the independent variable and those which act as confounding influences.[8] In non-

6. Notice that we are not dealing, here, with comparisons such as those between large and small cities, which may have quite different rates based on different individual suicides. Our comparisons would involve the same suicides, grouped together in different ways.

7. The basic problem is to separate the effects of the sociological correlates of size (e.g., anonymity, heterogeneity) from the purely statistical effects of grouping cases together artificially. For example, we might gain some insights by comparing suicide rates of cities of size 100,000 with the artificially constructed "pooled" rates for groupings of ten cities of size 10,000 each.

8. Leslie Kish, "Some Statistical Problems in Research Design," *American Sociological Review*, XXIV (June, 1959), 328-38.

experimental studies where randomization has not been possible, the most satisfactory procedure is to introduce explicit controls for as many of the latter variables as is possible. In order to do so, we must of course identify and measure such variables.

In our subsequent discussion we shall have to assume that all such potential confounding influences have been brought under control, though we shall comment briefly on the nature of complications introduced by these variables that are related to the independent variable X. All variables actually being controlled will be ignored by assuming that we are dealing only with that portion of the variation in the dependent variable which remains unexplained by these control variables.

We are then left with a single independent variable X, a dependent variable Y, and a number of unknown or unmeasured variables U, V, and W, which are conceived as causes of Y but which are unrelated to X. The causal picture can be represented as in Figure 13. For simplicity, we shall again assume linear models and no interaction effects.

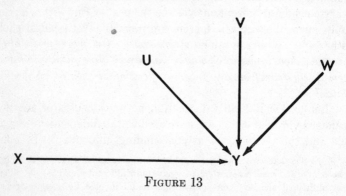

Figure 13

As already emphasized, the magnitude of the correlation coefficient is merely an indicator of how well we can predict from X to Y. Its numerical value depends not only on the amount of variation in the independent variable X but also on the degree to which variables such as U, V, and W have been brought under control. Were we able to control for these latter variables the correlation between X and Y should increase, whereas the value of b_{yx} should remain unchanged except for sampling errors.

This difference in the expected behavior of r_{xy} and b_{yx} can be seen if we substitute the predicted relationship $b_{ux}=r_{ux}=0$ into the equations for $r_{xy.u}$ and $b_{yx.u}$. Thus

$$|r_{xy.u}| = \frac{|r_{xy}-r_{ux}r_{uy}|}{\sqrt{1-r^2_{ux}}\;\sqrt{1-r^2_{uy}}} = \frac{|r_{xy}|}{\sqrt{1-r^2_{uy}}} \geq |r_{xy}|$$

and $$b_{yx.u} = \frac{b_{yx} - b_{yu}b_{ux}}{1 - b_{ux}b_{xu}} = b_{yx}.$$

In the case of $r_{xy.u}$ we see that the higher the correlation between U and Y, the greater the increase in r_{xy} produced when we control for U.

Variables such as U, V, and W can be thought of merely as nuisance variables, the effects of which should be controlled in order to obtain a better estimate of the slope. Were the slope to change as controls for such variables are introduced, scientific generalization would be next to impossible. But it should certainly come as no surprise that controls for U, V, and W would increase the correlation between X and Y. Indeed, this is as intended. Our interest in the magnitude of r is only as an indicator of how well we have estimated the slope or as a measure of how much error or dispersion we have.

What can we say about what will happen when we shift units of analysis? Suppose, for example, we were to pair off each of our cases, computing mean X and Y values for each pair, thus ending up with half as many units as before. What would happen to r_{xy} and b_{yx}? Unfortunately, the answer depends on *how* the units have been put together. In many practical instances, it is difficult to say very precisely how such units may have been grouped. For example, one state may be subdivided into a large number of small counties, whereas a second may consist of less numerous larger counties. From the standpoint of the social scientist, the decision to subdivide a state in one manner rather than another can be considered arbitrary. The smaller and more numerous counties in the first state might just as well have been grouped into clusters, just as we have imagined ourselves pairing off cases above.

Presumably, we are apt to combine spacial units according to geographical proximity. In so doing, we may affect the variation in the independent variable X. But we may also affect the variation in U, V, and W, and therefore in Y. Just how much the relative variations are affected, however, depends upon exactly how the criterion for grouping (e.g., proximity) is related to each of the variables under consideration. Usually we will lack this crucial information.

In order to gain insights into the nature of possible grouping effects, it will be useful to ask what we can expect to happen when we change our units of analysis in *known* ways that may be approximated, to varying degrees, by ordinary methods of grouping units. In particular, we shall consider three artificial ways of combining cases: (1) randomly, (2) so as to maximize the variation in X, and (3) so as to maximize the variation in Y. Other artificial groupings could also be made. For example, we might combine the units so as to minimize the variation in either X or Y. But, as we shall argue later on, most real-life groupings would seem to involve some combinations of these first three ways of forming artificial groupings.

Our original data consist of correlations and slopes computed for 150 Southern counties. These 150 counties, which cannot themselves be subdivided because of lack of data, will be taken as the original units of analysis.[9]   We shall form artificial groupings of increasing size. First, counties will be grouped into 75 pairs, then into 30 groups of 5 counties each, then into 15 groups of 10 counties, and finally into 10 groups of 15 counties. For each grouping we compute a mean X and a mean Y. We then obtain the values of r_{xy}, b_{yx}, and b_{xy} and note the changes in these coefficients as we move in the direction of a smaller and smaller number of increasingly large units.

We shall select two variables for which there is an original correlation (where $N = 150$) that is only moderately large (.54).

9. These "original" units of course vary in size in exactly the manner described. But they will be treated as all having the same initial weight.

Table 4. Comparison of Correlation and Regression Coefficients for Various
Methods of Grouping Data.

Method of Grouping	Measure	Un-grouped (N=150)	Grouped by				
			Pairs (N=75)	Fives (N=30)	Tens (N=15)	Fifteens (N=10)	
Random	r_{xy}	.54	.67	.61	.62	.26	
	b_{yx}	.26	.36	.31	.27	.18	
	b_{xy}	1.10	1.23	1.23	1.39	.37	
By X	r_{xy}	.54	.67	.84	.88	.95	
	b_{yx}	.26	.26	.26	.26	.26	
	b_{xy}	1.10	1.70	2.69	2.97	3.44	
By Y	r_{xy}	.54	.67	.87	.91	.95	
	b_{yx}	.26	.41	.68	.75	.84	
	b_{xy}	1.10	1.11	1.10	1.11	1.07	
By Proximity	r_{xy}	.54	.63	.70	.84	.81	(.77)
	b_{yx}	.26	.27	.28	.28	.34	(.29)
	b_{xy}	1.10	1.48	1.77	2.52	1.91	(2.05)

The X variable, which for the present we shall take as independent, is per cent nonwhite. The Y variable involves a measure of the differential between white and nonwhite incomes. The original value of b_{yx} is .26, indicating that a change in X of one unit corresponds to a change in Y of .26 units. Since we shall allow for the possibility that X rather than Y should be taken as dependent, we shall also comment on the numerical value of b_{xy}.

The values of the three coefficients for the several size groupings and for various methods of grouping the original units are given in Table 4. We shall now examine each of these methods in turn, beginning with random combinations of counties.

Random Groupings. If we group counties together on a random basis, we would ordinarily expect that most groups will contain some members with high X scores and some with low. When we compute the various means of these X scores, we thus expect to find less variation among these means than among the original 150 counties.   But we would also expect reduced variation in the U, V, and W scores, if these could be measured. And a reduction in the variation of these other causes of Y should mean a comparable reduction in the variation in Y.   Since grouping is completely random, we expect that the variations in both X and Y will therefore be reduced in accordance with the Law of Large Numbers.   Except for sampling fluctuations, we expect X to continue to explain the same *proportion* of the variation in Y, though the variation in both variables will decrease as we move in the direction of larger and larger units.   The value of r_{xy} should remain unchanged, except for sampling error.   Likewise, the covariance should decrease in the same proportion as the variances in X and Y, meaning that the expected values of both b_{yx} and b_{xy} should also be constant.[10]   Notice that since we are grouping randomly without regard to either X or Y, the behavior of the two regression coefficients is the same, no matter which variable is taken as dependent.

Reading across the top set of figures in Table 4, we see that for random groupings the data confirm our expectations.   Because of the relatively small number of initial units, the number of "cases" of grouped counties becomes quite small, and sampling errors are therefore considerable.   But taking simple arithmetic means for the four different-sized groupings, we see that the mean value of r is .54, that for b_{yx} is .28, and the mean b_{xy} is 1.06.   These values are quite close to the original figures of .54, .26, and 1.10 respectively.

We may conclude, then, that if units are grouped completely randomly, there should be no systematic effects on the magnitudes of any of the three coefficients.   This will be true regardless of the size of the groupings.   Needless to say, random groupings are seldom found empirically.   Nevertheless, we may

10. These facts can be seen from formulas given in Goodman, "Some Alternatives to Ecological Correlation," *Am. Journ. of Soc.*, p. 621.

use random groupings as a basis for comparison with other methods. Since there will usually be at least some element of randomness in any grouping procedure, we can consider most real groupings as involving a composite of random methods and one or more other methods, two of which will be discussed below. It can be expected, then, that empirical results will ordinarily fall somewhere between those predicted for random groupings and those that should occur under other "pure" types of groupings.

Groupings by X. Suppose we now put the original counties together so as to maximize the variation in the independent variable X. We rank the counties according to scores on X, pairing off the two counties with the lowest X scores, those with the next lowest scores, and so forth until we finally come to the two counties having the largest X values. Similarly, we group together the five counties having the lowest X scores, the five with the highest X's and so on. Finally, we group together 15 counties at a time in the same manner. We then compute mean X's and Y's for each group and compute four sets of coefficients, one for each size class.

In forming these artificial groupings by the X variable we are of course approximating what might be done in obtaining a regression equation with a much larger number of cases. Since the regression of Y on X represents the path of the means in Y for fixed values of X, we imagine an entire distribution of Y scores for each particular value of X. Here, the X values vary slightly within each grouping since only a relatively few counties have exactly the same X scores. But the value of X is almost being held constant within each grouping, and consequently the variation in X between groupings is at a maximum, being almost as great as among the original 150 counties.

But the variation in U, V, and W between groupings should be considerably reduced. Furthermore, the larger the groupings the greater the reduction in variation in each of these variables. Since these variables are assumed to be completely unrelated to X, the variable by which the original units have been grouped, we expect essentially random variations in U, V, and

W within each of the groupings and relatively small differences between the means of U, V, and W for these groupings.   In causal terms, the effect on U, V, and W of grouping in this manner is exactly the same as under random grouping.   Within each grouping, the effect of each of these variables will be canceled out according to the laws of probability theory.   These variables will thus produce less variation in Y, their "nuisance" effect will be lessened, and X, whose relative variation has been only slightly decreased, will explain a higher proportion of the variation in Y.

As the size of the grouping increases, therefore, the numerical value of r should also increase.   As can be seen from Table 4, not only does r in fact increase, but it does so steadily and rapidly, so that for groupings of size 15 the value of r is .95, meaning that approximately 90 per cent of the variation in Y is associated with X.   In essence, U, V, and W (whatever they are) have been effectively controlled in the grouping process.

Notice, however, that the numerical value of b_{yx} remains remarkably constant as the size of the groupings increases.[11] This is in accord with causal expectations and our research aims. *In controlling in this manner for variables that are unrelated to X, we do not expect the nature of the relationship between X and Y to change, though we do expect the sampling error of our estimate of the slope to be reduced.*

But the value of b_{xy} does not remain fixed, and in fact increases more rapidly than does r.   Mathematically, this can be explained in terms of the fact that $r^2 = b_{yx}b_{xy}$.   Obviously, if b_{yx} remains constant, then b_{xy} must increase in proportion to r^2. While this is a mathematical triviality, we must still account for it in causal terms.   We must remember that we are presently considering X to be the independent variable.   Therefore, we would not ordinarily be interested in the value of b_{xy} which is an estimate of the regression of X on Y.   For the time being, we merely note the trend in b_{xy}, with the realization that this particular coefficient would have been of interest had the roles of X

11. Although it is not apparent from the table, these slopes are not all exactly equal, since differences appear in the third decimal place.

and Y been reversed. But in this latter case, X would be taken as dependent, and we would have been grouping by the dependent rather than the independent variable. Let us now consider what can be expected to happen when we do in fact group by the dependent variable, which for simplicity we shall again take to be Y.

Groupings by Y. Suppose we group by the dependent variable Y in the same manner that we grouped by X. In effect, then, we maximize the variation in Y. Since the variation in X will be reduced more than the variation in Y, at first glance it seems plausible to expect that X should explain a smaller proportion of the total variation in Y. If so, the value of r_{xy} should decrease as we move in the direction of larger units.

Looking at the actual data, we see that as we go from left to right across the table the value of r increases in much the same fashion as it did when we maximized the variation in X. In other words, *r behaves symmetrically with respect to X and Y; no matter which one is used for purposes of grouping, r increases.* Mathematically, this is as expected, but it still requires explanation in causal terms. We note also that while b_{xy} remains constant as we go across the table, the value of b_{yx} increases roughly in proportion to r^2. Again, we might argue that since we have simply interchanged the roles of X and Y, we should now expect b_{xy} to behave the same way as did b_{yx}. But the apparent simplicity of such an explanation masks an important difference between the two situations.

We must remember that we are still considering Y to be dependent causally on X. Therefore, our primary interest focuses on b_{yx} rather than b_{xy}. Why should b_{yx} increase sharply when we group by Y, whereas it remained constant when we grouped by X? In grouping by X, we have essentially controlled out or minimized the effects of nuisance variables U, V, and W. Relative to X, their variation has been considerably reduced. But in grouping by Y we by no means reduce the variation in U, V, and W relative to that in X. Instead, we *confound* the effects of these nuisance variables with those of X.

Why should this be the case? Let us consider the group-

ing in which we have put together extremely high values of Y.
In order for Y to be very high, we must ordinarily have high
values in X *and* high values in variables such as U, V, and W,
assuming without loss of generality that all variables are positively related to Y. If we group together cases with high Y
scores, we would usually expect to find both high X's and high
U's. When we compute means in order to get a single X score
or U score for the group as a whole, we are likely to find a high
$\overline{X}$ associated with a high $\overline{U}$.

Similarly, in combining cases with low values of Y, we also
put together low X's, U's, and V's. This will be true even
where originally there was no tendency for X to be correlated
with any of these variables. *In grouping by Y, we are confounding the effects of all these variables, this being the very opposite of the
direction in which we usually wish to move. Almost any variable
that is even slightly related to Y initially becomes a good predictor of
Y under such a grouping procedure because of the fact that its effects
are being confounded with those of the other variables related to Y.*

Additional data illustrate this confounding of X and U. We
add a variable U (percentage of females in the labor force) that
has a low correlation of .08 with X (per cent nonwhite) using
the original 150 counties. Also, U initially has a moderately
low correlation of .38 with the dependent variable Y. As we
move in the direction of larger and larger groupings by Y, this
correlation increases from an original value of .38 to one of .88
for groupings of size 15. But, also, the correlation between the
two "independent" variables increases to .77, so that their
effects seem hopelessly confounded.

Causally, we would interpret the increase in the slope b_{yx} as
a reflection of the fact that other causes of Y have been confounded with the effects of X. Because of this, an increase in
X of one unit is linked with increases (or decreases) in the values
of these other variables. We are not, then, examining the relationship between a unit change in X and the change in Y holding other variables constant. Instead, we are doing just the
opposite, and by no stretch of the imagination can we simply

assume that the effects of these other variables in some way or another cancel each other out. It would thus be erroneous to take the numerical value of b_{yx} at face value.

Therefore, while X and Y behave symmetrically in the mathematical sense, the causal interpretations are quite different depending on whether we have grouped by the independent or the dependent variable. If we always take Y as dependent, then our interest should focus primarily on the value of b_{yx}. As we have seen, the numerical magnitude of r_{xy} should increase as we increase the size of our groupings. If we have grouped by X, the value of b_{yx} remains constant, subject to sampling errors. This is in accord with our scientific aims. But if we have grouped by Y, the value of b_{yx} will increase even more sharply than r_{xy}. In the former case we are reducing the effects of nuisance variables; in the latter we are confounding their influences with that of the independent variable X.

It is quite clear that there are a number of important implications of this fact stemming from our lack of knowledge, in real situations, of whether or not we are in effect grouping primarily according to X or to Y. If the former, we feel relatively safe in using b_{yx} as a comparative measure. But in the latter case, we will be in considerable difficulty.

Before taking up our final grouping procedure that is designed to approximate real-life groupings more closely, we must make several additional comments concerning the implications of groupings by X and Y. First, it should be apparent that in spite of our very different interpretations of these two situations, *since b_{yx} and b_{xy} behave symmetrically, we cannot make inferences as to the direction of causality on the basis of what happens to these two coefficients. Where direction of causality is not known, we do not know whether we have grouped by the independent or the dependent variable, nor do we know whether our interest should center on b_{yx} or on b_{xy}.* All we know is that *if* we have grouped by the independent variable, the coefficient in which we are really interested should remain fixed, whereas if we have grouped by the dependent variable, the value of the proper coefficient will reflect the influence of other variables that have been confounded with the independent variable. But we still may not know which variable is which.

Likewise, it should be made quite clear that if there happens to be a variable with a confounding influence in the original data, then grouping by the independent variable will not eliminate its effects but will continue to confound this variable with the independent variable.

For example, suppose that Z is a cause of both X and Y and that therefore its influence is originally confounded with that of X. If X and Z are positively related, then by grouping together large X values, we shall also group Z's together in a similar manner. In fact, looking only at the relationship between X and Z, we will be grouping by the dependent variable, thereby increasing the correlation between X and Z. Since Z also is presumed to cause Y, the value of b_{yx} will reflect the influence of Z on Y as well as that of X. Therefore, we cannot rely on grouping procedures such as we have been discussing to reduce the effects of confounding variables. *Grouping by X can only be assured of reducing the effects of "nuisance" variables as long as these latter variables are unrelated to X in the original data.*

Finally, we should note that had U, V, or W been known, we might just as easily have grouped by one of these variables. Suppose, for example, we group by U. Then, clearly, the correlation between U and Y should increase. But since U and X are unrelated, grouping by U is equivalent to grouping the X scores randomly. The variation in X will thereby be decreased, much more so than the variation in Y. Since the effects of X are not now confounded with those of U, however, we can expect the numerical value of r_{xy} to decrease. The expected value of b_{yx} should remain the same, although as the size of the groupings becomes large the sampling error in our estimate of the slope will become so large that the numerical value of b_{yx} will fluctuate widely from sample to sample, and whatever weak relationship may exist within the sample will probably not be statistically significant. In grouping by U, we are in effect doing exactly the opposite of what we intend to accomplish in an experimental design: we reduce the variation in the independent variable X while maximizing the influence of the nuisance variable U.

Groupings by Proximity. Empirical groupings were also formed on the basis of the physical proximity of counties, in much the same way that counties might be grouped into subregions or states. Since the original 150 counties represent only about one quarter of all Southern counties, only a relatively small number are actually adjacent. In grouping these counties into clusters of 2, 5, 10, and 15 counties each, a rather crude effort was made to select counties that were relatively close together within a state, or, in some cases, across state boundaries. The method of grouping was admittedly very imprecise, but it is probably not too dissimilar to that used in administrative decisions of various kinds. In other words, no attempt was made to find "natural" or sociologically meaningful groupings of homogeneous clusters. Needless to say, groupings were made without a knowledge of either the percentage of nonwhites X or income differentials Y.

An examination of the bottom set of figures in Table 4 indicates quite clearly the trends involved. The numerical value of r_{xy} increases across the table, though not nearly so sharply as in the case of groupings by either X or Y. The value of b_{yx} remains constant, except possibly for the last column. But b_{xy} increases, though again not as rapidly as was true for the groupings by X. It appears as though grouping by proximity represents a procedure that is intermediate between grouping randomly and grouping by X. The drop off in the values of r_{xy} and b_{xy} in the last column may be in part owing to the fact that when we put together as many as 15 counties, only a few of which are actually adjacent to any of the others, the groupings are beginning to become quite heterogeneous and more nearly random than is the case when only 2 or 5 counties have been grouped by proximity.

Thus we should probably not attach too much significance to the fact that the figures in the last column differ from what we would expect if the trends were to continue. For comparative purposes, we have placed in parentheses the appropriate figures based on groupings of the 150 counties into 10 states.[12] It can be seen that the results for states are quite similar to those for groupings of size 15 each.

In grouping by proximity we are apparently coming more closely to a grouping by X than by Y. But this may very well be a function of the particular variables we have selected as independent and dependent variables. Historically, certain geographical conditions of climate, soil, and rainfall may have in large part determined which areas were most suited for slavery. Assuming that counties that are physically close to each other tend to be similar geographically, we would also expect these counties to be similar with respect to per cent nonwhite, even though there has been a gradual dispersal of the minority group since the time of slavery. If we then take per cent nonwhite as a cause of discrimination, which in turn causes differentials between white and nonwhite incomes, proximity is more closely linked to per cent nonwhite than to differentials.

In other instances, however, a grouping by proximity might approach more closely a grouping by the dependent variable. In this latter case, we might be badly misled by the numerical value of b_{yx} which would then increase with the size of the grouping. Perhaps a series of empirical studies, using different sets of independent and dependent variables, might help determine whether in general we can expect that grouping by proximity will be more similar to grouping by independent variables than by dependent variables. If this should turn out to be the case, we might feel more comfortable in assessing the values of slopes in instances in which units are put together in such a manner. In the absence of such information about various types of independent variables, perhaps all we can do is to be extremely cautious in our interpretations.

Some Further Implications. At the risk of being repetitious, we again introduce a word of caution with respect to the in-

12. The sample does not contain an equal number of counties from each state, the range being from thirty-three counties in Georgia to eight in Alabama. This inequality is of course in part a function of the unequal sizes of the counties.

terpretation of correlation coefficients. We must recognize that in shifting units of analysis we are likely also to affect the degree to which other uncontrolled factors may vary. Notions of how important a variable is usually involve the *amount* of variation in that variable, as well as the nature of any relationships it may have with other variables.[13] Therefore, *in shifting units we may also vary the degree to which any particular variable is considered "important."* Variables that are important for one set of units may not be important for another.

We have seen how it is possible, by an artificial combination of units, to obtain a correlation of .95 between per cent non-white and income differentials. For these particular groupings, per cent nonwhite is obviously more important than any other variable, since we have manipulated the situation in such a way that the effects of most other variables are canceled out. In other words, our nuisance variables no longer vary. But with other combinations of units, the correlation between X and Y may be much less, and in fact we may find other variables that are more "important." Had we been able to group by U, then undoubtedly U would have been more important than X. We immediately see that there is a basic problem in evaluating relative importance.

A major implication of this property of correlation coefficients is that we must be on guard against committing a *Durkheimian type of fallacy*. The mere fact that suicide *rates* may vary from country to country, or by religious denomination, does not mean that "psychological variables" can be ruled out theoretically, in general or for any other types of units. We might even obtain extremely high multiple correlations for units such as cities, meaning that practically all of the city-by-city variation in suicide rates can be accounted for by so-called "ecological variables." This may be possible precisely because the units have been grouped in such a way that personality variables canceled out, being similarly distributed in all cities. But like-

13. See H. M. Blalock, "Evaluating the Relative Importance of Variables," *American Sociological Review*, XXVI (December, 1961), 866-74.

wise, a psychologist might have grouped his units by personality types in such a way that individuals' place of residence and other sociological variables did not vary from unit to unit.

Finally, it should be pointed out that in many instances where groupings have been made according to geographical or physical criteria (e.g., by states, communities, societies, neighborhoods), we might generally expect to find at least some correlations that are considerably larger than those found using persons as units. Not all correlations using groups as units will be large, of course. *But finding a high correlation does not demonstrate the superiority of sociological or ecological variables over others. It may merely mean that, as a result of the grouping operation, we have controlled out the effects of other variables. If* this is realized, we may take advantage of these grouping effects to help us better understand the nature of the relationships among factors that remain as real variables. But we should avoid jurisdictional disputes about which variables are "really" most important.

COMPARISONS WITH SAME UNITS, DIFFERENT VARIATIONS

Suppose that we are interested in comparing two samples involving the same kinds of units but which happen to differ with respect to the amount of variation in the independent variable. If we found a higher correlation between X and Y in the one sample than in the other, we might be tempted to infer an interaction effect: that the relationships between X and Y are inherently different in the two populations. In the extreme case, we might find no statistically significant relationship in one sample and a strong relationship in the other. And this might even be true where the two samples were of equal size. But in the first sample, there might be very little variation in X, whereas the second sample might be quite heterogeneous with respect to the independent variable.

Essentially the same type of argument can be used in this kind of situation as applied to comparisons involving different kinds or sizes of units. The numerical value of r_{xy} is a reflection not only of the nature of the relationship, as measured by a slope, but of the *amount* of variation in the independent variable relative to variation in any nuisance factors that may also be affecting Y (but that are again assumed unrelated to X). One may have deliberately manipulated the variation in X by either oversampling or undersampling extreme cases. In so doing, he will not ordinarily affect the variation in factors such as U, V, and W, but he will change the variation of these nuisance variables *relative to* that in X. In general, the greater the variation in X, the greater the magnitude of r_{xy}. But we do not expect the value of b_{yx} to be affected, except for the fact that the greater the variation in X, the more precise our estimate of the population slope, i.e., the less the sampling error in b_{yx}.

We are assuming that a manipulation of the variation in X has no bearing on the variations in U, V, and W because X is operating independently of these variables. Again, in most realistic situations it will be difficult if not impossible to decide the degree to which such unmeasured variables are in fact also being manipulated. For example, in deliberately selecting cases or in redefining his population, the researcher may inadvertently control for one or more nuisance variables by restricting their variation. Since we are supposing U, V, and W to be unknown or unmeasured, it will of course be impossible in real-life comparisons to assess the degree to which two populations may differ with respect to variation in these nuisance variables. Once more, however, we can see what happens when we manipulate the data artificially so as to form samples that differ from each other in known ways. We can then discuss certain practical implications for analyses based on real samples.

There is no need to form as many different types of groupings as was done in the previous section, as our basic types of results will be similar in nature. Clearly, if we were to subdivide the original 150 cases into two samples by completely random procedures, we would expect that in the long run there should be no systematic effect on the numerical values of r_{xy}, b_{yx}, or b_{xy}. Likewise, we would expect to find comparable results if we were to assign counties to one or the other sample on the basis of Y

Table 5. Comparison of Correlation and Regression Coefficients for Samples
with Differing Amounts of Variation in the Independent Variable X.

Measure	Total Sample $(N=150)$	High Variation Sample $(N=75)$		Low Variation Sample $(N=75)$
r_{xy}	.54	.64		.34
b_{yx}	.26	.27		.25
b_{xy}	1.10	1.53		.48
	Total Sample $(N=150)$	High Variation Sample $(N=50)$	Medium Variation Sample $(N=50)$	Low Variation Sample $(N=50)$
r_{xy}	.54	.70	.43	.15
b_{yx}	.26	.27	.24	.25
b_{xy}	1.10	1.78	.76	.09

scores as we would obtain by assigning on the basis of X scores.
As before, the values of X and Y would simply be reversed, although our causal *interpretations* would be quite different. We
shall therefore present data only for the case in which we assign
counties on the basis of X scores.

For our first comparison, we have grouped the counties into two samples of 75 cases each. The first sample was formed
by taking the 25 cases with the lowest X scores, the 25 with the
highest X scores, and a random sample of 25 from the remaining
100 counties. The second sample consists of the other 75
counties. Thus we have artificially made the first sample much
more heterogeneous on X than the second. The first contains
all of the most extreme cases plus a sampling of 25 intermediate
counties. The results are presented in Table 5 (top set of
figures).

Our second comparison involves three samples, the first of
which consists of the 25 most extreme cases at each end, the
second containing the 25 next most extreme in both directions,

and the third involving the middle 50 cases. These comparisons are given by the bottom set of figures in Table 5.

As we see for both sets of figures, the more heterogeneous the sample with respect to X, the larger the numerical value of r_{xy}. However, we do not achieve anywhere near the high degree of predictability between X and Y as we did when we grouped the data into new units. The basic reason seems to be that in forming these several samples we do not reduce the disturbing effects of the nuisance variables. All we can do is to increase the variation in X in the case of the first samples in each set of figures. Since there is a definite upper limit to this increase in the variation in X relative to variation in U, V, and W, we do not obtain correlations approaching unity. In other words, *we expect generally to find greater predictive power in instances where we can effectively reduce the variations in nuisance variables than in situations in which we can merely increase somewhat the variation in the independent variable.*

The important point about the results in Table 5, however, is the fact that *once more we find the numerical values of b_{yx} being relatively similar*, subject of course to sampling fluctuations. But the numerical values of b_{xy} are quite different. If, in fact, Y were actually the independent variable, then our interest should focus on b_{xy}. We would then be assigning the counties to samples on the basis of variation in the dependent variable, and again we would argue that the effects of the independent variable (now Y) are being confounded with those of whatever variables are operating on X independently of Y.

Our reasoning is the same as before. If X is caused by Y together with some other variable, say Z, then by selecting extremely high X scores, we are likely to be taking counties that are high on both Y and Z, if the relationship between X and Z is also positive. Similarly, in order for a county to have an extremely low X score, it is more than likely that it will be low on both Y and Z. Counties having high Y but low Z scores (or vice versa) will be underrepresented. *Thus counties that are extreme on the dependent variable X are likely to be ones in which Y*

*and Z are operating in the same direction. Their effects will be
confounded, so that the numerical value of b_{xy} reflects the influence
of Z as well as that of Y.*

Generally, the implications are clear. We must first of all
be cautious in interpreting results in which comparisons are
made involving samples with different degrees of variation in
either X or Y. If we are unwilling to assume a direction of
causation we must be doubly cautious. If we can assume that
we have only manipulated the variation in the independent variable X, then we can expect the value of b_{yx} to be unaffected
except for sampling error. Our interpretations should be based
on the size of this slope, rather than on the size of the correlation
coefficient. For example, if we suspect that the nature of the
relationship between X and Y is inherently different in two
populations, we should compare the sizes of the two slopes b_{yx},
rather than the magnitudes of the correlations.

A major advantage in comparing slopes, as contrasted with
correlations, is that even though two samples may not differ
significantly with respect to variations in the independent variable, they may do so with respect to unknown nuisance variables. If one sample happens to be more heterogeneous with
respect to such variables, the size of r_{xy} will be relatively smaller,
but the magnitude of b_{yx} should be unaffected, except that the
sampling error will be large. It should be noted, however, that
if any confounding variables are operating, we cannot eliminate or even estimate their effects on the size of b_{yx} unless they
can be either measured or controlled through randomization.
Once more we must always make certain simplifying assumptions about the effects of outside variables. We are presently
assuming that such confounding variables have negligible effects.

Occasionally, one finds in the literature instances in which
an author selects out only the extreme cases for analysis, although such a procedure has often been criticized. From the
previous discussion, it should be apparent that *it makes a considerable difference whether extreme cases are selected according to
the independent variable, or whether the dependent variable has
been used instead.*

If the researcher selects only the extreme cases with respect to his dependent variable, he will be confounding the effects of several independent variables. For example, if he takes only those persons with very high or low prejudice and then attempts to evaluate authoritarianism as a cause of prejudice, not only will r_{xy} be higher than with random sampling but the numerical value of the slope will also be misleading. If both authoritarianism and status-consciousness are causes of prejudice, and if both relationships are positive, then persons who are extremely high on prejudice are likely to be high on *both* independent variables, persons who are high on one independent variable and low on the other being excluded. *The practical result will be the exaggeration of the influence of the independent variable.*

Comparisons with Categorized Data. Because of the crude form of much of our data, and perhaps because of the inherent nature of certain of our variables, social scientists have often tended to make more use of either categories or ranked data than of interval scales, Pearsonian correlations, and regression coefficients. The use of lower levels of measurement does help one avoid making dubious assumptions about his units of measurement or about the normality of his frequency distributions. Under these circumstances, the use of crude categories is not only less pretentious but also would seem to result in fewer misleading interpretations.

But there is a serious shortcoming in the use of categories in instances where we conceive of the underlying variable as ordered but where measurement has been only very crude. Our choice of cutpoints is often quite arbitrary or, if not arbitrary, is determined by considerations of frequency distributions. Persons may be categorized as having either "high" or "low" prejudice, or as being either "conservative" or "liberal." Or they may answer a given item as either "Yes" or "No," such a response for some persons with intermediate attitudes being determined by the exact wording of the item in question.

Commonly, if scores are dichotomized they are cut somewhere near the median in order to provide a sufficient number of cases in each category. But in so doing, we may quite easily

Table 6. Comparison of Samples with High and Low Variation in the Independent Variable, Using Dichotomized Data.

| | Sample 1 (High Variation in X) | | | | Sample 2 (Low Variation in X) | | |
| | X | | | | | X | | |
	Low	High	Totals			Low	High	Totals
Y Low	31	14	45	Y Low		26	19	45
Y High	6	24	30	Y High		11	19	30
Totals	37	38	75	Totals		37	38	75

$$\chi^2 = 17.21$$
$$p < .001$$
$$\phi = .48$$
$$b_{yx} = .47$$

$$\chi^2 = 3.21$$
$$p > .05$$
$$\phi = .21$$
$$b_{yx} = .20$$

obscure the fact that there may be very real differences in variation from sample to sample. For example, suppose we were to dichotomize both the X and Y scores for each of the two samples of 75 counties discussed in connection with the top set of figures in Table 5. The results would be such as given in Table 6, where we have selected certain arbitrary cutpoints. These results appear quite different for the two samples, as measured in terms of both percentage differences and measures of association such as ϕ (phi). We have completely obscured the fact, however, that there is considerably more variation in X in the first sample than in the second. Incidentally, since the two samples differ less on variation in Y, we have in one sense done less injustice to the Y scores than the X scores. But if we were simply to look at the data in Table 6, knowing nothing else, there would be no way of telling whether or not this were the case.

Previously, in comparing these same two samples of 75 counties we saw that whereas the degree of relationship was not the same in both cases, the values of b_{yx} were similar. We argued that this is as expected, always allowing for the possibility of sampling error. In other words, the nature of the relationship is the same in both samples. But how can this be shown from Table 6?

As is well known, we can treat attributes as special cases of interval scales by simply assigning the values of 0 and 1 to low and high scores on both X and Y. We then find that the coefficient ϕ becomes a special case of r_{xy}. Likewise, it can be shown that if we take percentage differences, both down and across, converting these to differences of proportions, we will then have measures that are analogous to slopes. In particular, if we compute proportions down so that they add to 1.0 and then take differences across, we will get numerically the value of b_{yx}.

Thus for sample 1

$$b_{yx} = 31/37 - 14/38 = .84 - .37 = .47$$

and similarly

$$b_{xy} = 31/45 - 6/30 = .69 - .20 = .49.$$

In this particular instance, the values of the two slopes (i.e., differences of proportions) are approximately the same. But this is a function of the marginal totals and will not generally be the case.

As was true for interval scales, we may also write

$$\phi^2 = r^2_{xy} = b_{yx}b_{xy}.$$

Obviously, then, when the two slopes are exactly equal the value of ϕ or r will be equal to that of the slope or difference in proportions. This will happen only when the two sets of marginal totals are identical.

We see from Table 6 that not only do the two r's differ but the values of b_{yx} differ as well. Owing to the small number of cases involved, such a difference might very well be attributed to sampling error. *But we no longer have any theoretical reason to expect the two slopes to be approximately equal.* By dichotomizing X close to the median in both samples we have forced

Table 7. Comparison of Samples with High and Low Variation in the Independent Variable, Using Three Categories for the Independent Variable.

| | Sample 1 (High Variation in X) | | | | | Sample 2 (Low Variation in X) | | | |
	X_1	X_2	X_3	Totals		X_1	X_2	X_3	Totals
Y_1	80	50	20	150	Y_1	40	100	10	150
Y_2	20	50	80	150	Y_2	10	100	40	150
Totals	100	100	100	300	Totals	50	200	50	300

Proportions in Y_1 .80   .50   .20   .80   .50   .20

$$\chi^2 = 72 \qquad\qquad \chi^2 = 36$$
$$\phi = .49 \qquad\qquad \phi = .35$$

them to have the same variation in X, even though this does not do justice to the data. In effect, we are considering all of the highs in both samples to be exactly alike on X, and similarly for the lows. We have turned two frequency distributions with very different standard deviations into what amounts to a bimodal distribution with only two values. What is even worse, we have forced the two samples to have exactly the same variance in X. It is of course not necessary that we impose such a restriction even with dichotomies, but in practice this is more than likely to occur.

For purposes of contrast let us consider what might happen if we were to divide the X variable into three categories instead of two. Since the data we have been using involve too few cases for proper comparisons of 3 × 2 tables, let us illustrate the problem with data, presented in Table 7, which are purely hypothetical. These data have been set up so that there is greater variability in the X categories in sample 1 than in sample 2.[14] In the first sample there are equal numbers of cases

14. The notion of variation is technically undefined in the case of categorized data, though we assume that its meaning is intuitively clear in the present example.

in all X categories, whereas the bulk of the cases in sample 2 are in X_2.

The data have been contrived so that the nature of the relationship between the two variables is the same, as measured by the differences among the proportions computed down the table but compared across. Thus, for both tables we see that of the cases in X_1, 80 per cent are in Y_1. Similarly, for X_2, 50 per cent of the cases in both tables are in Y_1. Finally, we see that only 20 per cent of the X_3 scores are in Y_1 in both tables. Converting these percentages to proportions and examining the differences involved, we obtain something analogous to b_{yx}, except that the notion of linearity or even direction of relationship becomes meaningless if the categories in X are not even ordered.

If we are taking X as the independent variable, it makes very good sense to consider the two samples as expressing the same nature of relationship. No matter how many cases we happen to have in each X category, we get the same proportion in each Y category. Since the amount of variation in the independent variable is assumed not to be caused by the dependent variable, we wish to compare the two tables in such a way that variation in X is irrelevant, just as we have previously compared results by examining b_{yx} as an indicator of the nature of the relationship between X and Y. Notice, however, that if we were to compare the two tables by means of either a measure such as ϕ or percentage differences computed across but compared down, then the results for the two samples would look quite different.

Presumably, the data for these two samples could only vary on X in the appropriate manner if we selected the same cutpoints for both samples. For example, individuals might have been scored crudely on some attitude dimension. Cutpoints on X might have been selected at scores above 73, those between 49 and 73, and those which are 49 and below. In such a case, the actual frequencies for the several X categories would be permitted to vary. A greater dispersion in X within sample 1 would be reflected in relatively more cases in the two extreme categories. But suppose both samples had been subdivided into three equal parts, with 100 cases falling into each X category. Then we have obviously "forced" the samples to have equal variability on X, and the results would appear quite different.

In most instances it will not be possible to categorize X and still retain differences in variation in X which are commensurate with the differences that might have been obtained with less crude measurement techniques. Generally speaking, the greater the number of categories that can be retained, the more likely that one can measure such differences accurately. *The simplicity and other obvious advantages of the* 2×2 *table should not blind us to its defects.*

COMPARISONS INVOLVING CHANGE DATA

If we take X to be the independent variable, we can either estimate the slope by comparing cases that differ on X and Y at a given point in time or we can obtain an estimate by analyzing change data. If we compute change scores in both X and Y over some unit of time, and if we can make certain simplifying assumptions about the effects of outside variables, we should get the same estimate of b_{yx} (except for sampling errors) as would be obtained from comparative data.[15] The simplifying assumptions amount essentially to the requirement that there be no confounding influences.

Whereas change data should yield the same estimates

15. Change studies, of course, usually differ in important ways from comparative studies, and somewhat different analysis techniques will be appropriate in the two instances. One may have to allow for delayed reactions, making it necessary to "lag" certain variables in order to infer causal relationships. The fact that change studies usually involve the *same* units at numerous different points in time introduces the problem of autocorrelation and the necessity of making use of alternative statistical procedures. The reader is referred to the econometric and statistical literature on time-series techniques. See also L. A. Goodman, "Statistical Methods for Analyzing Processes of Change," *American Journal of Sociology*, LXVIII (July, 1962), 57-78; T. W. Anderson, "Probability Models for Analyzing Time Changes in Attitudes," in P. F. Lazarsfeld (ed.), *Mathematical Thinking in the Social Sciences* (Glencoe: The Free Press, 1954), Chapter 1; and D. T. Campbell, "From Description to Experimentation: Interpreting Trends as Quasi-Experiments, " in C. W. Harris (ed.), *Problems in Measuring Change* (Madison: University of Wisconsin Press, in press).

of b_{yx} as do comparative data, this is not to say that we expect the values of r_{xy} and b_{xy} to be comparable. Since our arguments will be essentially the same as before, we can keep our discussion relatively brief. Again, the magnitude of r_{xy} will depend not only on the size of the slope but also on the amount of change in X relative to that in nuisance variables such as U, V, and W. In experimental situations, one's aim is to create a relatively large change in the independent variable and to keep changes in nuisance variables to a minimum. In so doing, it is hoped that one can maximize r_{xy} and obtain a reliable estimate of the nature of the relationship, as measured by b_{yx}.

But when we deal with "natural" change data in which none of the variables are purposefully manipulated, values of X may change only very slightly over the time period covered. For example, if little migration occurs, the percentage of nonwhites in a county may remain relatively constant during a particular decade. Then, if a good deal of migration occurs in the next decade, substantial changes in X may suddenly occur. Comparable changes may or may not take place in the values of nuisance variables. Whereas the numerical value of b_{yx} may remain relatively stable from one decade to the next, the magnitude of r_{xy} may vary considerably according to the degree of variation in X, U, V, and W.

Thus we would generally expect temporal comparisons involving correlation coefficients to be less meaningful than those which make use of slopes. But again, we must watch out for possible "manipulations" of the dependent variable. One way of maximizing changes in X would be deliberately to compare only those units that have undergone a rapid change in X in one direction with those that either have undergone no change or that have changed the most in the opposite direction. In so doing, we would of course be overweighting extremes, thereby obtaining a higher correlation but a more accurate estimate of the slope. But if we were to overweight the extremes on the dependent variable, we would again be confounding the influence of the independent variable with the effects of nuisance variables. For example, by selecting those cases having a maximum change in Y, we are also likely to be overweighting units that are high on several causes of Y (assuming positive relationships) at the expense of those for which changes in the various independent variables are pulling in opposite directions.

CONCLUDING REMARKS

Without repeating what we have said about each of the specific types of comparisons discussed above, we should once more emphasize the principal point. *In nonexperimental studies of various sorts we are likely to find certain counterparts to experimental manipulations. But since these manipulations have often not been consciously made by the investigator, who may indeed be quite unaware of their existence or unable to measure their effects, we must be even more cautious in interpreting the results of these nonexperimental studies.*[16]

If there is any degree of assurance that in effect manipulations have been made primarily in terms of the independent variable, then comparisons involving slopes will ordinarily be more meaningful than those using correlation coefficients. This point is well worth emphasizing in view of what appears to be an overreliance on correlation coefficients in the sociological and psychological literature. Basically, our interest in correlation coefficients in these comparisons should be mainly to help us determine the degree of accuracy in our estimates of slopes.

But we have seen, also, that if in fact manipulations have been carried out primarily in terms of the dependent variable, then slopes are even more subject or sensitive to these manipulations than are correlation coefficients. Both types of coefficients are likely to create misleading interpretations, however. Since statistical manipulations of the dependent variable would seem to have few if any operational counterparts in the experimental situation, interpretations based on such manipulations should be made with extreme caution.

16. This same point is also emphasized in I. M. Towers, L. A. Goodman, and H. Zeisel, "A Method of Measuring the Effects of Television Through Controlled Field Experiments," in *Studies in Public Communication*, No. 4 (Chicago: University of Chicago Press, 1962).

V

Complicating Factors

In previous chapters the necessity of imposing a number of simplifying assumptions has been emphasized. We have assumed one-way causation, linear and additive models, the absence of confounding effects from outside variables, and negligible measurement errors. It has also been necessary to include in the theoretical system only those variables that have been directly linked with operational procedures. Many of these assumptions are highly restrictive. We must now raise important questions as to how we would proceed if one or more of these assumptions could be relaxed.

It would be highly encouraging if lifting these restrictions would lead to more or less straightforward extensions. Unfortunately, however, this does not appear to be the case. The social sciences are severely handicapped by the inability to experiment, imprecise measurements, and the difficulty in finding isolated systems for which the number of variables can be sharply delimited. We have already briefly mentioned certain problems encountered when one allows for reciprocal causation. We saw that coefficients may become unidentifiable unless additional information can be supplied. Likewise, we mentioned the problem of interaction for which nonadditive models would be more appropriate.

In the present chapter we shall discuss certain possible lines of attack on relatively simple problems where we must deal with (1) distortions produced by outside confounding influences, (2) unknown random and nonrandom measurement errors, and (3) models in which some of the variables must be taken as unmeasured. In each case we shall encounter rather formidable problems for which there appear to be no simple solutions. The approaches we shall suggest are obviously highly exploratory and as yet have not been applied to realistic problems.

Let us turn first to confounding influences. Later discussions of measurement errors and unmeasured variables will make use of similar approaches. *The general strategy will be to conceive of confounding influences, measurement errors, and unmeasured variables in terms of specific causal models in which we include not only the measured variables of direct interest but also unknown or unmeasured variables which may be taken as the sources of confounding effects or measurement error.* Certain of the variables included in the causal model will in each case be unmeasured, and our task will be to make inferences that either bypass or involve controls for these unmeasured variables.

REDUCING THE EFFECTS OF CONFOUNDING INFLUENCES

The scientific method can be viewed from the standpoint of the necessity of convincing the skeptic, who may raise a number of questions about the findings of any piece of research. Some of these questions may be illegitimate in the sense that they cannot possibly be answered definitively or even in probability terms. But others may be quite proper. One such question, which will be the focus of the present section, concerns the possibility that a relationship between two variables may be affected by an unknown third variable. Perhaps a social scientist has found a relationship that he asserts to be causal and not spurious. The study may or may not have been strictly experimental. Presumably, the investigator wants to establish that some independent variable X is an important cause of a dependent variable Y. He reports that as X is changed experimentally, Y tends to change also. Or he finds a high correlation between the two variables. The results are tested for significance, and it is found that it would be highly unlikely that they would occur under the null hypothesis of absolutely no relationship. But the skeptic may always raise the possibility that had some other variable been controlled, the results would have been otherwise.

In a sense, the objection of the skeptic is unfair if stated in vague terms. For no matter how careful the study, it is always possible to assert that some unknown and mysterious variable, which has been uncontrolled, is operating as a confounding influence in the sense that it is upsetting the "true" relationship between X and Y. Furthermore, it will be empirically impossible to show such an objection to be false. There is a burden on the skeptic at least to name the confounding influence involved, and ideally he should attempt to measure it and design an alternative study in which the presumed confounding influence is controlled.

But the entire burden should not be on the skeptic, whose question is basically quite legitimate. In the social sciences there are obviously large numbers of intercorrelated variables that are spuriously related, and as pointed out previously one of our most difficult and important tasks is to find valid ways of ignoring the myriad of spuriously intercorrelated variables in favor of the much smaller number of meaningful causal relationships. It therefore is of paramount importance to anticipate this particular kind of objection of the skeptic and to reduce the number of confounding influences to a minimum. There are, of course, several well-known methods for doing this, and we need only mention these briefly.

Let us take as our prototype of confounding influences the simple causal situation represented in Figure 14, where V and Z are operating (jointly) to produce a spurious relationship between a supposedly independent variable X and the dependent variable Y. This is in contrast with Figure 15, where T and U are taken as additional causes of Y but are assumed unrelated to X. In this latter situation, T and U will produce variation in

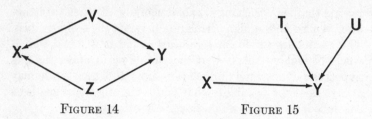

FIGURE 14   FIGURE 15

Y, but this variation will be independent of that caused by *X* and, from the standpoint of the investigator, can be taken as random.

One of the most desirable ways of eliminating the effects of confounding influences is to introduce explicit controls for these variables. There seems to be little disagreement about this point, although we should perhaps emphasize R. A. Fisher's argument that the application of several simultaneous controls for factors such as *V* and *Z* may be highly inefficient from the standpoint of cost considerations.[1] The obvious difficulty, in addition, is that such confounding influences may not even be identified, much less easily measured.

Fisher's alternative, of course, is randomization. In contrast with the first alternative involving rigid controls for confounding influences, we have seen that randomization does not control for these variables. But it makes them independent of *X*, except for sampling errors that can be evaluated in probability terms. Through randomization, variables such as *V* and *Z* are transformed into factors such as *T* and *U*. They continue to operate on *Y*, but they do not systematically affect the estimate of the relationship between *X* and *Y*, as measured by a slope. Since they continue to produce sampling error, however, randomization is in one sense a poor man's substitute for rigid controlling procedures.

A third type of alternative is to change the nature of the design, ideally as much as possible, and to replicate the study. For example, certain types of confounding influences in experi-

1. R. A. Fisher, *The Design of Experiments* (6th ed.; London: Oliver and Boyd, Ltd., 1951), Chapter 1.

mental studies may have only short-run effects (e.g., memory effects owing to repeated testing).   Others may not operate over short periods (e.g., effects of major outside events).   Hopefully, if both long-term and short-term experiments give very similar results, we might infer the nonexistence of these particular types of confounding influences.

Better still, the results of experimental studies might be contrasted with comparative studies involving data collected at a single point in time.   It is sometimes believed that change studies are generally superior to comparative ones.   It is true that change studies may give insights into temporal sequences, but another apparent advantage is in the superior control over confounding influences.   There is the suspicion that these latter influences may be more operative in comparative studies.   However, this all depends on how many variables are changing at once.   Obviously, change studies involving large numbers of variables, all of which are changing more or less simultaneously, admit the possibility of numerous confounding influences.   But we will have additional faith in the conclusions if two studies, one of which involves change data and the other comparative data, both give similar results.   Presumably, the same confounding influences are less likely to be operative in both studies.

Obviously there is no single procedure that will always guarantee the elimination of all confounding influences, and it will therefore be impossible to counter the skeptic's objections in a completely definitive way.   The investigator is always limited by funds and available knowledge and therefore seldom will be in a position to make use of alternative designs.   The procedure we shall suggest should be evaluated in the same light. It will not always work, nor will it be feasible in all pieces of research.   It is merely one among a number of possible alternatives for reducing the effects of confounding influences.   But in view of the fact that one of the social scientist's most thorny problems is to eliminate such variables, we need to examine as carefully as possible the potentialities of whatever techniques we have.

Grouping and Confounding Influences.   In the present sec-

tion we shall deal with what appears to be a new technique for reducing the effects of confounding influences. The discussion
will be limited to the rationale of the method, which will be applied to some artificially constructed data. Its full implications,
especially as applied to real data, remain to be explored.

Basically, the procedure involves artificial manipulation of
the data in such a way that the amount of variation in Z, the
confounding influence, is reduced relative to the variation in
the independent variable X. In other words, we attempt to
hold the confounding influence as constant as possible, rather
than to make it unrelated to the independent variable, as is ac-
complished through randomization. In essence, then, we treat
the confounding influence as a control variable. But the principal advantage of the proposed technique over conventional
controlling procedures is that we are not required to measure or
even identify the disturbing influences. Ideally, the method
can be used to reduce the effects of several confounding variables even when they are operating in completely unknown
ways. In practice, however, it will be helpful if the investigator
can anticipate the nature of the major confounding influences
and roughly how they operate.

The method again involves grouping the data into artificially contrived categories and then working with the *means*
of each category, rather than with the scores for individuals.
In so doing, we take advantage of the Law of Large Numbers,
which indicates that greater accuracy and less sampling error
will be obtained with macroscopic variables (i.e., means). The
trick is to group cases so as to reduce the effects of possible
confounding influences without simultaneously reducing the
effects of the major independent variable X.

In Chapter IV we assumed that all other causes of Y were
unrelated to X, so that in grouping by X we tended to cancel
out their effects. But what if there exists a confounding influence Z that not only affects Y but that is also a cause of X?
To be specific, suppose Z is positively related to both X and Y.
When we put together cases with large X values, these same
individuals will also tend to have high Z scores, and similarly

for those with low X values. Relative to variables that are unrelated to X, we will be increasing rather than decreasing the proportion of the variation in Y explained by Z.

As can easily be shown, the larger the groupings the greater the correlation between X and Z, and the more hopelessly confounded the effects of the two variables become. The numerical value of b_{yz} remains unaffected, as we saw in the previous chapter, but we cannot determine the magnitude of the component of this slope which is owing to the confounding influence Z. In other words, grouping by the independent variable helps to remove the effects of nuisance variables unrelated to X but not the effects of confounding influences. The method enables us to *predict* Y from X more satisfactorily, but it does not shed new light on the nature of the causal relationship.

But what if we can find a variable W that is a cause of X but that is unrelated to the confounding influence Z? If we now group so as to maximize the variation in W, we shall also maintain a higher degree of variation in X than would be expected by chance. If W and X are positively related, large X's will tend to be grouped together into the same categories as contain the largest W's. But the Z's will be randomly distributed throughout the various groupings, thereby considerably decreasing the variation among the $\bar{Z}$'s. Furthermore, the larger the size of each group the less the variation in the $\bar{Z}$'s relative to that in the $\bar{X}$'s. As a result, Z will be held virtually constant and its confounding effects thereby reduced. This will of course be true for any confounding influence that is unrelated to W.

In practice, it will be difficult to find W's that are completely unrelated to all confounding influences, although some degree of assurance can be obtained if one can group separately by several different causes of X, obtaining essentially the same results each time.[2] It therefore becomes necessary to examine what can be expected to happen when W is weakly or moderately

2. Essentially the same kind of strategy is suggested by Curtis and Jackson with respect to the use of multiple indicators. See R. F. Curtis and E. F. Jackson, "Multiple Indicators in Survey Research," *American Journal of Sociology*, LXVIII (September, 1962), 195-204.

related to Z, keeping in mind the fact that Z will be unmeasured and perhaps even unrecognized.

The Data. Before considering several specific causal models in detail, some comments are necessary concerning the nature of the empirical data we shall use. Unfortunately, the adequacy of the method cannot be assessed empirically with real data for the simple reason that we are dealing with unknown or unmeasured variables. To be sure, we could select variables that appear to be interrelated in accordance with some particular causal model. But in so doing we would have to assume the nonexistence of confounding influences, the very factors whose effects we are attempting to study. Since these variables may be operating in unknown ways, there will be no way of empirically evaluating the method with real data.

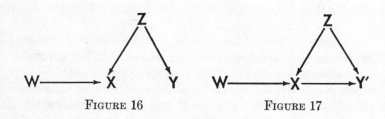

FIGURE 16   FIGURE 17

We have therefore made use of a device that may also prove useful in other circumstances. Artificial data for 160 "individuals" were constructed so as to conform to the linear causal models indicated in Figures 16 and 17. A table of random normal numbers was used to assign values to W and Z. These variables are independent of each other except for sampling error and are normally distributed with unit variances. Values of X were then determined from the regression equation:

$$X = 3W + 4Z + e_1$$

where e_1 is also normally distributed. Variation in X, which will be taken as the major "independent" variable, comes from three sources: (1) W, which will be used as the causal variable according to which individuals are grouped; (2) Z, which will be taken as the confounding influence; and (3) a number of other sources which have been lumped together as e_1 but which are assumed to have effects that are uncorrelated with W and Z.

We have similarly constructed Y and Y', which will be used as "dependent" variables. The regression equations for these variables are as follows:

$$Y = 3Z + e_2$$
$$Y' = X + 3Z + e_2$$
$$= X + Y.$$

Notice that neither of these variables is directly caused by W, the variable we shall use for grouping purposes. Both dependent variables are identical except for the fact that Y' depends causally on X, whereas Y does not. The relationship between X and Y is completely spurious due to Z; that between X and Y' is only partly spurious. The effects of all other variables are summed up in e_2, which is also normally distributed and independent of the remaining variables.

Our basic problem is to take out the effects of the confounding influence Z without actually controlling for this variable explicitly. But since we know the value of Z we can partial it out by standard techniques, comparing results with those of the grouping operation. We would of course expect the values of $r_{xy.z}$ and $b_{yx.z}$ both to be zero. Actually, because of sampling errors in the original 160 random numbers, we obtained $r_{xy.z} = -.09$ and $b_{yx.z} = -.07$. Since we shall have to consider these 160 cases as constituting our "population," it is these latter values, rather than zero, which we shall use as our standard for purposes of comparison. Without the control for Z, the value of r_{xy} is $.37$, and the value of b_{yx} is $.33$. In other words, the effect of the confounding influence is to change the slope from $-.07$ to $.33$ or a total shift of $.40$, and to raise the correlation from an insignificant negative value to one that might be described as "moderate" by most social science standards.

We shall also wish to consider the relationship between X and Y'. Since we have constructed Y' to be exactly $X + Y$, the

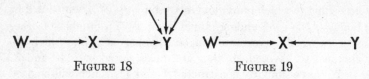

slope of the relationship between X and Y' will be exactly 1.00 greater than the value of b_{yx}. Therefore $b_{y'x}=1.00 + .33=1.33$ and $b_{y'x.z}=1.00 + (-.07)=.93$. Had there been no sampling error, the latter partial slope would of course have been exactly 1.00. But whereas the slopes b_{yx} and $b_{y'x}$ are related in this simple manner, the correlations are not. The value of $r_{xy'}$ without a control is .86. Controlling for Z we get $r_{xy'.z}=.70$, indicating that X explains about half of the variation in Y' remaining after the effects of Z have been removed.

We shall now assume that Z cannot be measured or possibly even identified. If the reader prefers, he may think of Z as representing the total effects of *all* confounding influences on both X and the dependent variable. It should be explicitly noted that we are working with linear models and that the data have been constructed accordingly.

Specific Models and Results. First consider the very simple model in which no confounding influence is assumed to operate. In Figure 18 the variable W by which we wish to group is taken as a direct cause of the independent variable X, which in turn causes Y. The small arrows leading to Y emphasize that there will ordinarily be a large number of other causes of Y, but we assume that their net effect produces variation in Y that is unrelated to the influence of X. What can we expect to happen when we group individuals so as to maximize the variation in W?

Unless the relationship between X and Y is nearly perfect, there should be a greater relative reduction in the dispersion of the Y means than of the X means. On a less intuitive basis, we know that the causal model of Figure 18 gives the prediction that $r_{wy}=r_{wx}r_{xy}$. Using this predicted relationship, we can substitute it into the equation for $r_{xy.w}$. It is then a simple matter to show that the magnitude of the total correlation between X

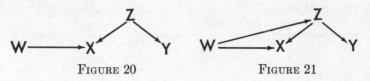

FIGURE 20   FIGURE 21

and Y should be greater than that of the partial controlling for W, if X and Y are initially imperfectly related. Thus $|r_{xy}| \geq |r_{xy \cdot w}|$. Similarly, we have seen that if the relationship $r_{wy} = r_{wx} r_{xy}$ holds as predicted, then a control for W will produce no change in the value of the slope b_{yx}. Therefore $b_{yx \cdot w} = b_{yx}$, except for sampling errors.

The model thus predicts that a control for W should decrease the strength of the relationship between X and Y but leave the slope unchanged. This is consistent with common sense. In *controlling* for W we are restricting the variation in X, while presumably not affecting any of the other causes of Y. We can therefore expect X to explain a smaller proportion of the variation in Y, but there is no reason to expect the slope to change. In *grouping* by W we are of course doing just the opposite of controlling for W; we retain as much variation in W as possible, while reducing variation in the other causes of Y. Grouping by W should increase the correlation between X and Y, but it should not affect the value of b_{yx}.

In contrast consider the two models represented as Figures 19 and 20, models that appear quite different but that yield the same predictions when grouping by W. Both of these models imply that there should be no correlation between W and Y, except for sampling error. Using this fact and inserting $r_{wy} = 0$ into the equation for $r_{xy \cdot w}$, we reach the conclusion that for both Figures 19 and 20, a control for W will increase the correlation between X and Y, i.e., $|r_{xy \cdot w}| > |r_{xy}|$, except in the trivial case where $r_{xw} = 0$. Therefore, when we group by W we should expect that the correlation will be smaller numerically than the original r_{xy}. In grouping by W, we are retaining most of that variation in X that is produced by a source (W) that is independent of Y and Z, while simultaneously reducing the variation

Table 8. Relationship between X and Y, and X and Y', Grouping by W That Is Unrelated to Confounding Influence Z.

		Original Data	Grouped Data			Partials
			by 4's	by 8's	by 16's	
Spurious	b_{yx}	.33	.21	.06	−.04	−.07
	r_{xy}	.37	.30	.12	−.11	−.09
Partly Spurious	$b_{y'x}$	1.33	1.21	1.06	.96	.93
	$r_{xy'}$	.86	.88	.91	.93	—

in Y and Z. Therefore Y and Z explain a smaller proportion of the variation in X.

But will the slope b_{yx} again remain constant when we group by W? Algebraically we can show that a control for W will increase $|b_{yx}|$ as well as $|r_{xy}|$, and therefore we can expect that grouping by W will have the opposite effect of decreasing $|b_{yx}|$. This result will hold for both models represented as Figures 19 and 20, but for different reasons causally. In Figure 19, Y is a cause of X, and it would make little or no sense to compute b_{yx}. Instead it is b_{xy}, the least squares estimate of the regression of X on Y, in which we should be interested. As argued in the previous chapter, the expected value of b_{xy} should not be affected if we group by W although there will be more sampling error in our estimate since we are in effect taking out much of the variation in Y.

It is in situations such as represented in Figure 20, however, where we should be theoretically interested in b_{yx}. Here, Z is producing a spurious relationship between X and Y, but in grouping by W we are reducing this spurious effect. The portion of the variation in X due to W is not being substantially reduced in the grouping process, but if we were to compute mean values of Z we would immediately note a reduction in the variation in this confounding influence. We are assuming, however, that Z has not been identified or measured.

The model of Figure 20 is of course the same as that for

Figure 16. Making use of our artificial data to test the effectiveness of the grouping operation, we obtained the results indicated by the top set of figures in Table 8. Grouping into categories of size 4 can be seen to have only a minor effect on both the correlation r_{xy} and the slope b_{yx}. But when we use groupings of size 16 the results are remarkably similar to those obtained earlier, when we assumed that it was possible actually to control for the confounding variable Z.[3] Focusing particularly on the slopes, we note a reduction from an original value of .33 to one of $-.04$, which is quite close to the "correct" value of $-.07$. *In grouping by W, we have very effectively taken out the influence of Z without having had to introduce an explicit control for this variable.*

The causal situation represented in Figure 17 is of course a combination of those in Figures 18 and 20. The relationship between X and Y' is partly spurious, and we have already indicated that for the particular data being used the direct influence of X on Y' should be measured by a slope of .93, whereas the apparent value (without a control for W) is 1.33. From the bottom set of figures in Table 8, we see that as we increase the size of the groupings we come closer and closer to this correct value. But this time the size of the correlation coefficient increases, rather than reducing to zero as in the case of complete spuriousness.

As we have indicated previously, the numerical value of this correlation coefficient has little meaning when we group in such a manner, except to indicate that we have effectively taken out most of the variation in Y' produced by all sources that are unrelated to W. Incidentally, it is no coincidence that the values of $b_{y'x}$ are always exactly 1.00 greater than those of b_{yx}, because this is the way the data were constructed. But the correlation coefficients cannot be compared in such a simple manner. Again we see that it is often more meaningful to examine slopes than correlations.

Grouping and Confounding Variables Not Independent. In

3. These partials have been inserted in Tables 8 and 9 for comparative purposes.

most real-life situations, we will of course not know how the confounding influence is operating. Furthermore, there may be several such variables. Therefore it is very important to ask what would happen if we were to group by a variable that happens to be related to the confounding influence. Would this not further confound its effects? The answer depends on how highly related the grouping and confounding variables happen to be. If highly correlated, then when we group so as to maximize the variation in W we also retain a high degree of variation in Z, perhaps relatively more than remains in the major independent variable X. The causal model involved might be depicted as in Figure 21, which is of course only one of many conceivable situations.

It is possible to derive mathematical inequalities concerning the relative magnitudes of the various correlation coefficients that will be necessary in order for a grouping operation to reduce, rather than increase, the confounding effects of an outside variable that is correlated with the grouping variable. However, most of the simpler inequalities that we were able to derive were rather weak in that they tended to underestimate the maximum size of the correlation between W and Z. Furthermore, these inequalities did not yield information concerning the magnitude of the gain (or loss) through grouping. It was therefore decided to investigate the matter empirically through the use of artificial data. A major shortcoming of such empirical procedures is, however, that one does not know how generally the results will apply.

The values of W were changed so that the correlation between the grouping variable W and the confounding influence Z was gradually increased. In so doing, we could not help but also affect the correlations between W and the independent variable X as well. The correlations of W with both Z and X are given in the first two columns of Table 9. The top row of figures represents the original data in which W and Z were independent $(r_{wz} = -.01)$. The figures in the bottom row of the main body of the table were inserted to show what happens when the correlation between the grouping variable and confounding influence

Table 9. Grouping by a Variable W That Is Related to Confounding Influence Z. (Size of Group = 8)

Correlation of W with		Size of Coefficient	
Z	X	b_{yx}	r_{xy}
−.01	.35	.06	.12
.08	.37	.08	.21
.17	.39	.14	.34
.26	.40	.23	.47
.42	.44	.25	.49
.59	.48	.32	.71
.88	.62	.48	.87
Original Values		.33	.37
Partials		−.07	−.09

is considerably higher than between the former and the independent variable. The value of $r_{wz} = .88$ is of course much higher than would usually be found in practice, assuming Z could be measured.

The crucial set of figures is in the third column, which indicates the effect of grouping on the slope b_{yx}.[4] Here we have grouped individuals into classes of size 8; presumably, the results would be more pronounced for groupings of size 16. The figures with which these slopes should be compared are, of course, −.07 and .33, the former being the "correct" slope and the latter including the influence of the confounding variable. We see that when r_{wz} is small, as compared with r_{wx}, we still gain quite a bit by grouping. For example, when $r_{wz} = .17$, the slope is reduced from the original .33 down to .14, or about half of the distance to the correct value of −.07. As the correlation between W and Z becomes moderate, we see that we do not gain much by grouping. However the surprising thing, to the writer at least, is that even when r_{wz} is as high as .59—higher than r_{wx}—

4. Notice that the values of $b_{y'x}$ can be obtained by adding 1.00 to b_{yx}, but there is no such simple way of inferring the values of $r_{xy'}$.

we still do not lose by grouping. On the other hand, in the bottom set of figures where $r_{wz} = .88$, we see that the confounding effect of Z has been further increased in the grouping process.

Notice that the effect of grouping on r_{xy} is more pronounced. Since the partial correlation with a control on Z is approximately zero, we would be badly misled if we were to group and then examine only the correlation coefficient. But as we have indicated previously, our focus of attention should be on the slopes rather than on correlations, which merely measure how well we can predict from the one variable to another.

Implications and Cautions. We have suggested a method for reducing the confounding effects of variables that operate as disturbing influences on a relationship between X and Y. As indicated earlier, there is certainly no guarantee that this procedure will always work, just as we cannot rely completely on any other devices such as randomization. It has been seen that *if we group cases together so as to maximize the variation in some variable that is a cause of the independent variable X, and if this grouping variable is unrelated (or weakly related) to the confounding variable, then the larger the size of the grouping, the more of the variation in the confounding influence that can be removed.* If we are primarily interested in establishing scientific laws and hence focusing on slopes, this grouping procedure should give us results that approximate those which would be obtained if the confounding influence could actually be controlled. It is therefore not necessary to identify or measure the confounding influence. In this sense, the grouping device has an advantage that is similar to that of randomization.

But there are obvious shortcomings and disadvantages of this method. Perhaps most significant from the practical point of view is the problem of finding a grouping variable W that can safely be assumed to be a cause of X without, at the same time, being either a cause of Y or related to the confounding influences. In the former case, grouping by W would mean emphasizing a variable (i.e., W) that is itself a confounding influence (since W is a cause of both X and Y). In the latter case, whereas grouping by W may remove the effects of some confounding influences, it may simultaneously increase those of others.

Obviously, the use of grouping procedures depends upon rather sophisticated analyses in terms of multivariate causal models. It may be argued that most social sciences are nowhere near ready to make use of such procedures. But we might just as well ask whether we can afford to ignore them since in most of our work randomization may be impossible, and yet there may be far too many confounding influences to be controlled explicitly. Nor can these confounding influences safely be ignored or dealt with in a cursory manner.

In view of these manifest difficulties, we would suggest two things. First, we must give considerable methodological attention to the problem in order to develop alternative ways of reducing the effects of confounding influences. To assess the adequacy of any given technique it may help to use artificial data, which can be modified and manipulated at will to approximate empirical situations but which can also yield "correct" standards for comparative purposes.

Our second suggestion is that *in actual empirical research the investigator should develop the habit of making use of alternative procedures in order to see if they give similar results.* Most effectively, he might compare outcomes using grouping techniques on cross-sectional data with, perhaps, those from an experimental study. At the very least, he might group by two or more different variables assumed to be causes of his major independent variable. *If several such W's give similar results, particularly if they are not too highly intercorrelated with each other, one may have added confidence that confounding effects have been reduced.* As in the case of other contrasting comparisons, if the results of separate grouping operations are quite different, new insights may possibly be obtained by asking why these specific differences have occurred.

MEASUREMENT ERROR IN NONEXPERIMENTAL STUDIES

The social science literature contains relatively few discussions of the consequences of measurement error or how suspected errors might be handled. Most of our attention has rightly been focused on how to improve measurement techniques so as to reduce such errors to a minimum. Quite obviously, a science cannot develop unless it can continue to improve its measurement procedures, and special attention must be given to problems of measurement during the exploratory phases of the science. But in any realistic piece of research, the social scientist must rest content with measurement that is imperfect to some degree. How will these errors affect his inferences and what, if anything, can be done to reduce their effects after measurement has already taken place?

Much of the literature in mathematical statistics assumes perfect measurement, except in the dependent variable. In applied statistics there are often discussions of how to handle random measurement error when the degree of such error can be estimated through repeated measurement. For example, if one has obtained as few as two measures on each individual, by using test and retest or split-half techniques, he may correct the values of correlations for attenuation.[5] Whenever repeated measurements have been made, such techniques are highly advisable. But suppose we are not in a position to estimate the amount of random error? Or—much worse—what if we suspect nonrandom errors but cannot assess their effects? All of the statistical sources familiar to the writer do not deal with such nebulous problems, though notes of caution are often introduced. Yet, unfortunately, unestimated random errors and biased measurements occur more frequently than not in practical research.

Our present purpose is to explore certain very limited facets of the general problem of measurement error, a topic that is highly complex and worthy of considerable research. In particular, we shall argue that it is helpful to conceptualize measurement error in terms of causal models. We shall suggest a procedure that may be useful, in some pieces of research, for reducing the effects of certain types of measurement error.

5. For a discussion of such corrections, see George A. Ferguson, *Statistical Analysis in Psychology and Education* (New York: McGraw-Hill Book Company, 1959), Chapter 18.

In the discussion that follows, the underlying variable being measured will be treated as distinct from the measure itself, which for convenience will be referred to as an indicator. We assume that there is, in a sense, a causal relationship between the two in that the correct value of the underlying variable is one among a number of causes of the recorded value of the indicator. For example, suppose one is attempting to measure a woman's age. The "age" that is actually recorded (i.e., the stated age) can be thought of as "caused by" the woman's actual age plus a number of other factors such as her own ignorance of the date of birth, a tendency to round off her age to even years or multiples of five, an effort to appear more youthful than is actually the case, or—in the case of elderly persons—a wish to appear over sixty-five so as to obtain social security benefits.

If the causes of measurement error are numerous and each relatively unimportant or applicable only to a small proportion of the cases, then the net effect of such causes is likely to be a close approximation to random errors. In the long run they can be expected to cancel each other out in the sense that mean values of the indicator will tend to be close to the mean of the true values. Thus although the ages of many individual women may be poorly estimated, the estimate of their mean age will be quite reliable.

Nonrandom errors, however, may occur in a number of ways. First, and simplest, there may be a constant source of error superimposed upon the random error. For example, all women might underestimate their ages by exactly three years. If so, the investigator would report the mean age incorrectly. But in relating age to some other variable the error would not appear in either a correlation coefficient or a slope, but merely in the constant a in the equation $Y = a + bX$. In other words, errors that are strictly constant can be ignored for certain purposes, including the making of causal inferences. In causal terms, we presume that factors that produce really constant errors are operative in the same way in all cases and hence are themselves constant and can be ignored in causal analyses. In our hypothetical example, we would be assuming that some variable is operating alike on all women to make them understate their ages by three years.

More commonly, however, nonrandom measurement error cannot be assumed to be of this constant variety. Only *some* women will underestimate their ages, and these particular women may not be equivalent to a random sample of all women. The tendency to distort may be related to other variables, including some which the investigator may wish to study. It is these nonrandom and nonconstant sources of error which of course create one of our most important types of faulty inferences. Incidentally, we cannot assume that measurement error is random merely because it is unrelated to the value of the variable being measured. Thus it is possible that the tendency to distort one's age is completely unrelated to this age (e.g., older women no more likely to distort than younger ones), and yet the tendency to distort may be highly related to some *other* variable (e.g., education).

In terms of causal diagrams, we shall represent the underlying or correctly measured variables as X, Y, and Z, and the measured values as X', Y', and Z'. The measured values will be taken as caused by the underlying variables plus certain factors t, u, and v, which are responsible for the errors in measurement. These latter variables will be related to the original variables in many ways, only a few of which will be examined.

Random Errors. For illustrative purposes let us consider the simple three-variable case of a spurious relationship in which Z causes both X and Y. Exactly the same results will occur when Z intervenes between X and Y. In other words, the models $X \leftarrow Z \rightarrow Y$ and $X \rightarrow Z \rightarrow Y$ predict the same results, even when we allow for random measurement error in all three variables. The situation can be represented as in Figure 22, where there are causal arrows connecting the underlying variables but none directly linking the measured indicators X', Y', and Z'. We have used t, u, and v to represent the total effects of all sources of random error on the respective indicators. Thus X' is conceived as being caused by X and t, and so forth. Linear additive models are assumed, and in the case of random measurement error the

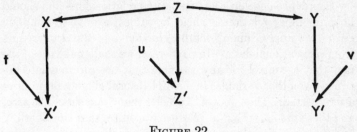

FIGURE 22

"variables" t, u, and v are taken to be independent of each other as well as the underlying variables.

Suppose first that we are primarily interested in the relationship between Z and Y. It is well known that if there is measurement error in the dependent variable Y but not in Z, the value of the correlation coefficient will be attenuated, but the expected value of the regression coefficient will be unaffected.[6] The introduction of random measurement errors in the dependent variable reduces the accuracy of our prediction, but it does not systematically affect the nature of the relationship, as measured by a slope. This is of course consistent with our expectations and, incidentally, is an advantage of slopes over correlation coefficients.

But if we also have random measurement error in the independent variable as well, the slope will likewise be attenuated. These facts are discussed in the statistical literature cited above and need not be dealt with in further detail. The question of immediate concern is whether or not random measurement errors will also lead to faulty causal inferences. In particular, we might ask whether or not a control for Z will completely wipe out the relationship between X and Y (as it should), even when there are random errors in each variable. We should note that it is entirely conceivable—if not plausible—that this may happen under certain conditions, since all correlations will be attenuated.

6. See especially J. Johnston, *Econometric Methods* (New York: McGraw-Hill Book Company, 1963), Chapter 6.

In order to develop a set of expected relationships that should hold among correlation coefficients, subject always to sampling errors, we apply Simon's method for making causal inferences from correlational data.   In particular, we shall make use of the fact that a control for any variable that lies intermediate between two other variables in a simple causal chain will produce a zero partial.   Thus we would predict that $r_{x'z \cdot x}$ should be zero, and therefore $r_{x'z} = r_{x'x}r_{xz}$.   Notice, of course, that since both X and Z are not directly measured, this particular relationship cannot be verified empirically.   Applying similar reasoning we get the following set of expected relationships:

$$
\begin{aligned}
r_{x'z} &= r_{xx'}r_{xz} & r_{y'z} &= r_{yy'}r_{yz} \\
r_{xz'} &= r_{xz}r_{zz'} & r_{yz'} &= r_{yz}r_{zz'} \\
r_{x'z'} &= r_{xx'}r_{xz}r_{zz'} & r_{y'z'} &= r_{yy'}r_{yz}r_{zz'} \\
&= r_{x'z}r_{zz'} & &= r_{y'z}r_{zz'} \\
&= r_{xx'}r_{xz'} & &= r_{yy'}r_{yz'}.
\end{aligned}
$$

From these basic equations we may derive several results. Let us first suppose that there is random measurement error in both X and Y but not in Z, the variable that falls intermediate in the causal chain $X \rightarrow Z \rightarrow Y$ and which is also "intermediate" in Figure 22 in the sense that it is directly linked to both X and Y.   We can now ignore Z', or if one prefers, we can consider $r_{zz'}$ to be unity.   Assume that we have computed the correlation between X' and Y', the two indicators of X and Y respectively. We wish to see if the relationship is spurious and we control for Z, assuming no error in the latter variable.   If the causal model of Figure 22 is correct, then we should have:

$$
\begin{aligned}
r_{x'y'} &= r_{xx'}r_{xz}r_{yz}r_{yy'} \\
&= r_{x'z}r_{y'z}
\end{aligned}
$$

or $r_{x'y' \cdot z} = 0.$

Thus we can expect that a control for Z will produce a zero partial except for errors introduced by sampling fluctuations. In effect, the relationships between X and Z, on the one hand, and Y and Z, on the other, have both become attenuated in such a way that the product of these attenuations exactly (except for sampling error) compensates for the attenuation in the relationship between X and Y. *If there are no measurement errors in Z, we can therefore expect the correct results when we control: the partial will be reduced to zero.* As can easily be verified, the same relationship should hold under the model $X \rightarrow Z \rightarrow Y$ where a control for Z could be used to interpret the relationship between X and Y.

But it is more than likely that there will also be measurement error in Z, in which case we must control for Z' rather than Z which will be unknown. Multiplying the correlations between X' and Z' and between Y' and Z' we get

$$r_{x'z'}r_{y'z'} = r_{xx'}r_{xz}r^2_{zz'}r_{yz}r_{yy'}$$
$$= r^2_{zz'}r_{x'y'}.$$

Therefore $\qquad r_{x'y'} = \dfrac{r_{x'z'}r_{y'z'}}{r^2_{zz'}}, \quad$ if $r^2_{zz'} \neq 0$

and $\qquad r_{x'y'.z'} \neq 0$

but $\qquad |r_{x'y'.z'}| \rightarrow 0 \quad$ as $\quad r^2_{zz'} \rightarrow 1.$

Here we see that the numerical value of $r_{x'y'}$ will generally be greater than the product of the correlations between Z' and the other two indicators. Strict equality will hold only when $r^2_{zz'}$ is unity, i.e., when there is no random measurement error in Z. The greater the measurement error in Z, the greater the inequality, and the further the partial will be from zero. In the extreme, when Z and Z' are completely uncorrelated, Z' will also be unrelated to X' and Y' (under the assumed model), and controlling for Z' will have no effect whatsoever on the correlation between X' and Y'.

The practical implications of these results are quite clear. *An investigator who is studying the relationship between two variables X and Y, and who is genuinely interested in testing for the possibility of spuriousness, cannot afford to be careless in his measurement of so-called "test" variables.* In fact, he will not be led astray by moderate random measurement errors in either X or Y, whereas he may if he measures a variable such as Z only very crudely.

As previously pointed out, the procedure of controlling for

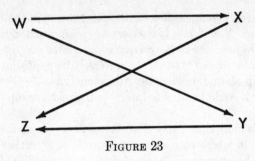

FIGURE 23

background or "demographic" variables is particularly vulnerable in this respect.   Often, factors such as sex, education, race, occupation of father, or religion are only very crude indicators of more important "experience" variables.   If used as controls, they cannot be expected to reduce a partial to zero, even when the relationship between X and Y is completely spurious.   In effect, this means that the investigator needs to pay careful attention to the measurement of his control variables, as well as the major independent and dependent variables under study. His *top measurement priority should undoubtedly go to the independent variable*, particularly when his attention is focused on slopes as contrasted with correlation coefficients, i.e., when he wishes to establish scientific laws rather than to estimate how well he can predict from one variable to the other.   In any event, *random errors in the dependent variable can perhaps be more easily tolerated than comparable errors in control variables.*

   There are, of course, many more complex situations than the three-variable case we have been considering.   In any given instance, it should be helpful to attempt to draw causal diagrams in order to assess the potential effects of measurement errors of various kinds.   For example we might have a four-variable model as in Figure 23.   As can easily be shown, the relationship between W and Z will be reduced to zero with simultaneous controls on X and Y only if there is no random measurement error in the latter two variables.   We can, however, tolerate random errors in W and Z and still have this particular partial reduce to zero.   But the model also predicts that $r_{xy \cdot w}$ should be zero, and this will occur only when there are no random errors in W. Therefore, in order for both predictions of the model to hold there can be errors only in the dependent variable Z, and these latter errors must of course be random.

Errors owing to Categorization. Whenever crude categories must be used with either nominal or ordinal scales, a certain amount of information is usually lost. The seriousness of such measurement error depends, among other things, on the number of categories. Where there is an underlying continuous distribution, a simple dichotomy does more injustice to the data than would three or four ordered categories.

Contingency methods of controlling are less efficient than adjusting techniques that, however, require simplifying assumptions such as additivity. When one wishes to control simultaneously for two or more variables by using separate tables, it often becomes necessary to work with dichotomies on the control variables unless the sample size is unusually large. Thus if one is to control for both occupation and religious preference, he may be confined to the four-fold distinction between white-collar Protestants, blue-collar Protestants, white-collar Catholics, and blue-collar Catholics.

As we have just seen, sizable random measurement errors in the control variables may result in the nondisappearance of a partial even when the original relationship is completely spurious and owing to these particular control variables. One then runs the risk of confusing spurious situations with other models. For example, as indicated previously, if we control for the background variable W in the model $W{\rightarrow}X{\rightarrow}Y$, the correlation between X and Y should be reduced though the magnitude of b_{yx} should remain unchanged except for sampling errors. Similarly, the situation where W intervenes, i.e., $X{\rightarrow}W{\rightarrow}Y$, might very well be confused with one in which X causes W and also Y, i.e., $W{\leftarrow}X{\rightarrow}Y$. With no measurement errors in W the relationship between X and Y should vanish completely in the former case, but the crude categorization of W might make it much more difficult to infer that W interprets the relationship between X and Y.

Unfortunately, the problem of evaluating the magnitude of distortions produced by categorization appears to be quite complex statistically. We have therefore resorted to several empirical tests involving artificial data for which it is possible to compare the behavior of total and partial correlations using interval scales, ranked categories, and simple dichotomies. Results for three separate samples, each involving 160 cases, can be reported quite briefly. In all samples linear models and normally distributed error terms were used.

In Sample I, X and Y were constructed so as to be highly correlated but spuriously related owing to Z. In the case of product-moment correlations, the original correlation was reduced from .57 to $-.01$ with a control for Z. Partial Kendall's tau's were computed by two methods: (1) by using the formula

$$\tau_{xy.z} = \frac{\tau_{xy} - \tau_{xz}\tau_{yz}}{\sqrt{1-\tau^2_{xz}}\ \sqrt{1-\tau^2_{yz}}}$$

and (2) by taking a weighted average of the tau's within categories of the control variable Z.

For the first method, four categories were used for each of the three variables. For the second, four categories were retained for X and Y, but Z was both dichotomized and divided into quartiles.[7] The original tau was reduced from .45 to .07 using the partial formula. Where four categories of the control variable Z were used, the weighted average tau was .04, whereas dichotomized Z scores gave a result of .16. Thus *in both cases where four categories of the control variable were used, the partial was reduced nearly to zero, whereas the use of two categories gave less satisfactory results.*

When all three variables were dichotomized and relationships measured in terms of ϕ's and percentage differences, the

7. These results were for tau$_c$, though very similar results were obtained using tau$_b$ and slope analogues. For discussions of tau, see M. G. Kendall, *Rank Correlation Methods* (New York: Hafner Publishing Company, 1955). For a discussion of slope analogues, see Robert H. Somers, "A New Asymmetric Measure of Association for Ordinal Variables," *American Sociological Review*, XXVII (December, 1962), 799-811.

original ϕ was only reduced from .45 to .20, and the results for percentage differences were almost identical. However, when the control variable Z was divided into quartiles, thus giving four 2×2 tables, the average ϕ was reduced to .04. Again we see the importance of retaining more than two categories in the control variable.

Sample II was constructed in order to investigate what would happen with the introduction of *two* simultaneous controls. X and Y were spuriously related owing to Z_1 and Z_2, which were taken as independent of each other. The total product-moment correlation between X and Y was .34, and this was reduced to .20 with one control and to .13 with both controls. For this particular sample the apparent effects of sampling error were more pronounced than with previous artificial data, and the reductions with categorized data must therefore be compared with the reduction from .34 to .13, rather than with the complete disappearance of the partial.

Partial Kendall's tau's were again computed by method (1) using four categories for each variable. The total association of .32 was reduced to .24 with one control and to .21 with simultaneous controls. In the case where all variables were dichotomized, the original value of ϕ was .32 and the first- and second-order partials were .29 and .26 respectively.[8] In the latter instance where both Z_1 and Z_2 were dichotomized, giving four 2×2 tables, the reduction from .32 to .26 was very minor and of the order of magnitude that might lead the investigator to infer that the original relationship was not spurious owing to Z_1 and Z_2.

From Samples I and II we see the very real advantages in keeping more than two categories for the control variables. The behavior of the partial tau's was intermediate between that of product-moment correlations, on the one hand, and that of average ϕ's with dichotomized controls on the other. In Sample II, we could also attempt to keep four categories for each control, giving sixteen 2×2 tables with an average of ten cases in

8. Results were almost identical using percentage differences, weighted average ϕ's, and partial formulas. Likewise, tau_b's and rank-order slope analogues gave results similar to those reported for tau_c's.

each table. The weighted average ϕ in this instance actually turned out to be .17, but since the number of cases in some tables was reduced to as low as four, we expect a high degree of sampling error in this figure. *It is precisely the combination of moderate-sized samples and several simultaneous controls which often forces the social scientist to resort to simple dichotomization of his control variables. In view of the results with Sample II, perhaps it would be less misleading to use either more categories and weighted averages or partial correlational formulas and standardizing techniques.*[9]

Sample III was formed in order to investigate partially spurious situations where the control variable should not be expected to explain all of the relationship between X and Y. The variables were constructed so that X was a direct cause of Y, with a unit increase in X producing a unit increase in Y. Superimposed on this was a partially spurious relationship owing to Z. Two cases were investigated: (1) where Z was positively related to both X and Y and (2) where Z was positively related to X but negatively to Y. In the first instance, the effect of Z was to produce a high total correlation between X and Y of .88 and a total slope of 1.57. In the second case, since Z operated so as to cancel a portion of the direct positive relationship between X and Y, the original correlation was .45 and the slope .43. With *product-moment* coefficients a control for Z produced a partial correlation of .64 in both cases, and—most important—gave partial slopes of .99 and 1.01 in the two situations. In other words, *regardless of the direction in which Z operated, a control produced the same end results*.

Results with ordered categories and dichotomies were by no means as satisfactory. In case (1) we of course expect to start with a much stronger total relationship between X and Y than in case (2), where Z is weakening rather than reinforcing this

9. In the case of unordered data with more than two categories, standardizing procedures would seem most appropriate provided additivity can be assumed. See Morris Rosenberg, "Test Factor Standardization as a Method of Interpretation," *Social Forces*, XLI (October, 1962), 53-61.

direct relationship. But with a control for Z relationships should be "brought together" if there is little or no measurement error in Z. Using Kendall's tau the original relationship was reduced from .73 to .49 in case (1) and raised from .30 to .34 in case (2).[10] The two partials of .49 and .34 were thus possibly sufficiently far apart to lead one to infer that the relationships between X and Y were actually different in the two cases. Slope analogues in this instance proved to be somewhat more encouraging, but differences between tau's and slope analogues were such that they might very well be attributed to sampling error.

For 2×2 tables the comparable changes in ϕ's were from .70 to .52 for case (1), and from .22 to .29 for case (2). Here, the final partial ϕ's of .52 and .29 were substantially different in spite of the fact that the two models were exactly equivalent except for the direction of the relationship between Z and Y.

While these empirical findings with artificially constructed data may not be really definitive, they indicate the need for further investigation and proper caution in interpreting results where data have been crudely categorized. In particular, as emphasized earlier, *the mere fact that the degree of relationship happens to decrease with the introduction of controls is by no means sufficient to distinguish among a number of alternative possibilities.* Unfortunately, also, it appears to be the case that slope analogues do not behave very differently from correlation analogues.

Nonrandom Errors. Nonrandom or systematic measurement errors may arise because of the fact that disturbing influences are introduced into the causal picture. Sometimes the investigator may reasonably suspect the operation of these influences and may even be able to predict the direction of their effects. He will be fortunate, scientifically, if they happen to be operating in the direction opposite to the one predicted by the theory. He can then claim that, had there been no measurement error, his results would have been even more striking in the

10. Again tau_b, tau_c, and alternative controlling methods produced almost identical results when four categories of each variable were used.

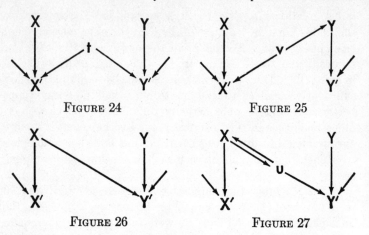

FIGURE 24   FIGURE 25

FIGURE 26   FIGURE 27

predicted direction.   But these same errors may also result in
no apparent relationship where, in reality, a relationship exists
between the actual variables under study.

Let us distinguish between two types of nonrandom errors,
those produced by variables that are unrelated to the independent variable X and those that are related to X in some way.
Examples of the first type are represented in Figures 24 and 25,
whereas those of the latter kind are given in Figures 26 and 27.
Needless to say, we are dealing with only the simplest of situations.   In particular, we are here taking X and Y as unrelated
causally but are supposing that the investigator finds a relationship between X' and Y' which he suspects is spurious and owing
to measurement error.   Since the possibility of spuriousness
may be evaluated against the alternative that X causes Y, we
can treat X as the "independent" variable.   Obviously, numerous other causal possibilities can be imagined, though it may
not be at all simple to trace out their implications.

In Figure 24 the cause of the measurement error in both X
and Y is a third variable t that is unrelated to both variables.
In Figure 25 the disturbing influence is a cause of the dependent variable but not the independent variable.   Figure 26
represents a situation where X is a cause of measurement error

in Y, but not Y itself. In Figure 27 the measurement error in Y is linked to X indirectly through u, which may be either a cause or an effect of X. In each instance there may be additional random measurement errors, as indicated by the small side arrows. In all four situations we would find nonvanishing correlations between X' and Y', and unless t, u, and v could be identified, measured, and controlled it might be extremely difficult to decide which model, if any, is the most appropriate.

It is hard to find "pure" examples of each type of causal situation. As an approximation to the model of Figure 24 or perhaps a combination of Figure 24 and Figure 25, we might consider the relationship between marital friction and delinquency. The former might be measured crudely in terms of divorce or separation rates, the latter in terms of numbers of arrests. Confining our attention to the lower classes, the race of the individual may in part determine the probability of arrest, given a delinquent act. But race may also be causally related, perhaps indirectly to be sure, to the chances of marital friction's resulting in divorce or separation. Negroes may have higher separation rates and arrests, without there being any real relationship between marital friction and "true" rates of delinquency. This fact might go unnoticed unless a control for race were introduced.

As an illustration of a disturbing influence such as indicated in Figures 26 and 27, suppose X is degree of urbanization and Y is job discrimination. The latter variable in particular cannot be measured directly. But suppose we take as an indicator of Y the difference between white and Negro incomes. Such a differential results from a number of factors besides discrimination, however, including the possibility that relatively more poorly educated Negroes than whites are attracted to cities. If so, we can imagine urbanization leading to differential migration (u), which in turn affects income differences between whites and Negroes. There may be no more discrimination Y in urban areas than rural ones, and yet the income differences Y' may be greater in urban centers.

In both of the above illustrations erroneous inferences could be avoided by the introduction of the proper controls.   Often, however, the investigator will not be in a position to control explicitly for the disturbing influence.   Curtis and Jackson propose another type of solution to the problem through the use of multiple indicators.[11]   In essence they suggest that one make use of several different indicators of both X and Y.   Instead of combining these indicators into a single composite index, as is commonly done, the researcher can gain valuable insights by keeping the indicators distinct.   Since it is unlikely that a single disturbing influence t, u, or v will operate in the same way on all indicators, we obtain a certain degree of insurance against making wrong inferences.   For example, if all of the indicators of X are related in the same way to all indicators of Y, then we have better evidence of a "real" relationship between X and Y. It should be noted that we are concerned, here, only with the problem of spuriousness owing to *measurement error*.   Such a use of multiple indicators will of course not take out the effects of any third variable Z that is a cause of both X and Y.

Our reason for distinguishing between situations in which the factor producing the measurement error is related to X and those in which it is not will become apparent in the next section. The procedure we shall introduce will work only in the latter instances (as in Figures 24 and 25).   It should be noted that the introduction of explicit controls for the disturbing influence and the use of multiple indicators will work in both types of situations.

Removing Measurement Error by Grouping.   When repeated measurement is possible, the scientist has a relatively simple device for reducing random measurement error.   He merely computes a mean score from a number of independent replications, making the assumptions that the property in question has remained constant from one replication to the next and that deviations from the true value are randomly distributed with zero mean.   In most social science research, of course, such repeated measurements are either impossible or rendered less use-

11. Curtis and Jackson, "Multiple Indicators," *Am. Journ. of Soc.*, pp. 195-204.

ful by the fact that the property being measured cannot be assumed to remain constant from one replication to the next.

Suppose, however, that we were to perform a mental experiment in which we assumed that the true scores of a number of individuals were known. Instead of taking repeated measures on the *same* individual, we might then perform a closely related operation. We might put together all individuals having the same true score, computing a mean of the measured scores for these persons. We would then expect the resulting mean to be relatively close to the true mean, and furthermore, the larger the number of "identical" individuals in each grouping, the closer the mean of the measured scores should be to the true score for these individuals. Statistically, we would be carrying out a procedure that is indistinguishable from that of repeated measurements on the same individual.

Such an imaginary experiment is of course impossible owing to our ignorance of the true scores, the very values we wish to estimate through measurement. But suppose we could find a variable W that is a cause of the variable X that we wished to measure. Assume that W can be measured perfectly, although it is sufficient that W be measured with random errors. If we group individuals together according to their scores on W, we should not expect them all to have identical X scores, even if they are perfectly alike on W. But if the other causes of variation in X and Y are unrelated to W, the effects of these other causes should cancel out if the size of each grouping is sufficiently large. This will also be true with respect to any variables producing measurement error in X and Y, *as long as these disturbing variables are unrelated to W.* Grouping by W should therefore take out measurement errors that are random and those that are owing to confounding influences unrelated to W and X.

In practice we cannot group together individuals who are identical on W. Instead we put together, say, the cases with the ten highest W scores, those with the next ten highest scores, and so forth until we come to the ten individuals with the lowest scores on W. If W is positively related to the independent variable X, there will be a tendency for high X scores to be grouped together, and for lows to be together. But within each grouping measurement errors should cancel out, there being approximately equal numbers of individuals whose errors are positive and negative. If we compute mean X and Y scores for each grouping, we can reduce the measurement errors in both variables. Because of the fact that we shall be using mean scores for each grouping, the numerical value of the correlation coefficient will have little practical meaning. But we can obtain a much better estimate of the true regression coefficient, which will no longer be as highly attenuated because of measurement error.

We cannot make use of real data to evaluate the effectiveness of this grouping procedure, since both measurement errors and real values will be unknown. Therefore we constructed artificial data generated by a table of random normal numbers and linear regression equations. The dependent variable Y was taken as $Y = 1.00\ X + e_1$ where e_1 was normally distributed and random. Because of sampling errors the actual value of b_{yx} was .97 instead of 1.00. The correlation between X and Y was a moderately high .78.

"Measurement errors" were next introduced by two methods: (1) by adding random variation to both X and Y and (2) by adding a confounding influence v creating a spurious relationship between the measured values X' and Y'. In the case of the random error, the estimate of the regression coefficient $b_{y'x'}$ reduced to .57 and the correlation to .56. For convenience we made the confounding influence operate in the same direction as the relationship between X and Y, producing a spuriously high relationship between the independent and dependent variables. The introduction of such a nonrandom measurement error raised the estimate of the slope to 1.35 and the correlation to .89.

The causal models, together with the values of r and b, are shown as Figures 28, 29, and 30. In Figure 28 we have the situation in which there is no measurement error. The value of the slope (.97) for this model serves as a standard to evaluate the effectiveness of the grouping technique. Figures 29 and 30 represent situations involving random and nonrandom measurement errors respectively. Incidentally, if we were to put to-

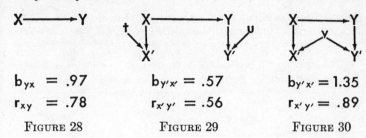

$b_{yx} = .97$	$b_{y'x'} = .57$	$b_{y'x'} = 1.35$
$r_{xy} = .78$	$r_{x'y'} = .56$	$r_{x'y'} = .89$
FIGURE 28	FIGURE 29	FIGURE 30

gether the two types of errors, we would expect them to compensate in that random errors produce attenuation whereas v, because all correlations are positive, happens to increase the relationship between X and Y. As it turned out, putting the two sources of error together gave $b_{y'x'} = .99$, but the similarity to the correct value of .97 is merely coincidental.

We constructed a variable W in such a way that W caused X (and therefore indirectly Y as well), but W was unrelated to t, u, and v, the sources of measurement error in X and Y. The total number of cases was 160, and "individuals" were put into groups of size eight and sixteen according to their scores on W. For example, the eight cases having the highest W scores were grouped together, as were the eight with the next highest W scores, and so forth. We then obtained mean scores on both X' and Y' for each of the groupings and computed the values of $b_{y'x'}$ for the various situations.

The results are given in Table 10. We see that for both random and confounding errors the distortions were considerably reduced in magnitude, especially in the case of groupings of size 16. Here the values of the estimated slopes were .89 and 1.04 as compared with the standard "correct" value of .97. Had there been enough cases to make use of groupings of size 32 or larger, measurement errors could have been reduced to negligible amounts.

Some notes of caution are again appropriate. The grouping procedure requires us to find a variable W that is a cause of the independent variable X, but that cannot be a direct cause of the dependent variable Y. If W happens to cause Y as well, then

Table 10. Effects on Slope b_{yx} of Grouping by W, Which Is a Cause of X but
Unrelated to Sources of Measurement Errors in X and Y. ($N = 160$)

Source of Measurement Error	Original Slopes (with error)	Grouped by 8's	by 16's	Correct Slope (no error)
Random	.57	.86	.89	.97
Nonrandom	1.35	1.11	1.04	.97

we shall be grouping by a confounding influence, and any gains
we make in reducing measurement error will be more than
compensated for by the fact that we will in effect be maximizing
the relative variation in the disturbing influence W, thereby
hopelessly confounding the effects of X and W on Y.

In practice, since it may be difficult to locate a single W
that we are almost certain possesses the desired properties, it
will ordinarily be sensible to attempt to group by several such
causes of X.   If we get essentially the same results each time we
do so, we may have added faith in our conclusions.   But if W_1
and W_2 give very different estimates of the slope b_{yx}, we would be
led to ask the significant question as to why this should occur.
Perhaps one of the W's will be related to the source of measurement error.   Or it may be a direct cause of Y.   In either instance, by grouping by several W's we may gain added insights
into the nature of the causal models and sources of measurement errors.

INFERENCES INVOLVING UNMEASURED VARIABLES[12]

Thus far the unmeasured variables we have considered have
been merely nuisance variables the influence of which we have
tried to control.   But in many instances these unmeasured variables may be important in their own right.   In fact, certain of
the measured variables may be much less significant theoreti-

12. This section represents a brief summary of the writer's paper, "Making
Causal Inferences for Unmeasured Variables from Correlations among Indicators," *American Journal of Sociology*, LXIX (July, 1963), 53-62.

cally and may be taken merely as indicators of the underlying variables. These latter variables may be of primary concern, and yet it may be almost impossible to measure them with any degree of accuracy. How can we handle such variables in terms of causal models if we wish to obtain predictions that are empirically testable?

It will be useful to make a distinction between an operational definition and an index or indicator. Certain theoretically defined variables can be readily associated with operations for measurement purposes. Thus age, sex, race, and religious membership need hardly be given theoretical definitions since their meanings are almost immediately apprehended. On the other hand, we have a number of abstract or vaguely defined variables: anxiety, values, prejudice, anomie, cohesiveness, and so forth. Until agreement has been reached among social scientists concerning appropriate operational definitions of these terms, we must perhaps treat them as unmeasured variables.

A causal model that contains a proportionately large number of unmeasured variables will be "top-heavy" in the sense that it will yield only a small number of empirical predictions relative to its complexity. This will of course mean that there are likely to be a large number of much simpler alternative models giving these same predictions. It will therefore be helpful if additional measured variables can be utilized, even where these latter variables are theoretically uninteresting in their own right. In particular, we may wish to associate one or more indicator variables with each unmeasured or underlying variable. Provided we can keep the causal model relatively simple, we may then arrive at a set of empirical predictions involving only the measured variables.

For our present purposes it will be useful to distinguish among three types of variables: (1) theoretically important variables that have been linked with operational definitions, (2) unmeasured theoretical variables, and (3) measured variables that are of little theoretical interest but that can be used as indicators of the unmeasured theoretical variables. We shall have to assume that each indicator variable is either a cause or an effect (but not both) of one and only one underlying variable. There may be several indicators of each unmeasured variable.

If we allow for the possibility that any given indicator is an effect (or cause) of more than one underlying variable, we shall run into difficulties when we attempt to make differential predictions concerning these underlying variables. Unless the latter variables can be linked simply with *other* indicators, the effects of the several underlying variables on their common indicator may be hopelessly confounded together.

For example, suppose we take suicide rates as an indicator of (1) anomie, (2) an overly strong attachment to the group, and (3) social isolation. We then create a theory that, from the standpoint of testability, is entirely too flexible unless we can introduce additional measured variables linked separately to each of the three underlying or unmeasured variables. Assume that we find an instance where suicide rates are high. We may attribute this to any one or more of the three unmeasured variables, selecting whichever one appears most plausible theoretically in an ex-post-facto analysis. While we would be doing a grave injustice to Durkheim to imply that his theory of suicide can be reduced to such simple terms, there does appear to be a certain degree of unfortunate flexibility to Durkheim's analysis.[13] We are suggesting that, at least in part, the difficulty stems from associating a particular indicator with more than one underlying variable.

Likewise, one should avoid complex indicators that are related in unknown ways to a given underlying variable. Geographical region and certain background variables appear to have such undesirable properties. For example, "education" as measured in terms of years of formal schooling would seem to stand in a very complex relationship to numerous attitudinal variables. On the one hand, it is a cause of these attitudes (at least those developed in later life), but on the other it is an effect of earlier socialization that may also be directly linked with these same attitudes. Although it may not always be possible to avoid the use of such complex indicator variables, the investigator should be alerted

13. Émile Durkheim, *Suicide* (Glencoe: The Free Press, 1951).

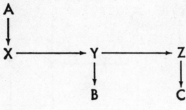

FIGURE 31

to possible misinterpretations owing to the complexity of the causal situation.

Examples. To take up a simple illustration suppose that we have three unmeasured variables X, Y, and Z and three indicator variables A, B, and C. Let A be a cause of X, and let B and C be effects of Y and Z respectively, as indicated in Figure 31. For example A may be race and X exposure to discrimination. We take the biological variable race as one among a number of causes of exposure to discrimination, and we assume the causal relationship is not reciprocal. X and Y, respectively, may be the two postulated psychological states "alienation" and "political liberalism." B and C may then be behavioral responses such as answers to a paper-and-pencil anomie test and voting behavior. We assume that voting behavior is caused (in part) by liberalism rather than the other way around.

The model of Figure 31 of course yields a number of predictions that cannot be checked empirically since X, Y, and Z cannot be measured. Among these predictions are the following:

$$r_{ab} = r_{ay}r_{by}$$
$$r_{bc} = r_{by}r_{cy}$$
and
$$r_{ac} = r_{ay}r_{cy}.$$

Multiplying together the first two equations, taking absolute values, and noting that $r^2_{by} \leq 1$, we obtain

$$|r_{ab}r_{bc}| = |r_{ay}r^2_{by}r_{cy}| = |r^2_{by}r_{ac}| \leq |r_{ac}|.$$

We are reduced to one prediction that is empirically verifiable. Obviously, it would be helpful to include additional

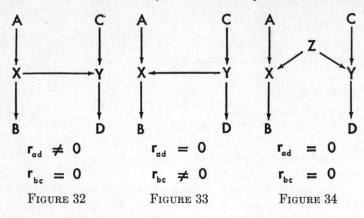

theoretical variables that are at the same time measurable, provided the model is not thereby made hopelessly complex.

For a second type of example we might consider situations in which we have two indicators of each underlying variable, one being a cause and the other an effect. Several simple causal models of this type are given in Figures 32-34. The three alternative models in Figures 32-34 can readily be seen to give different empirical predictions among the measured variables A,B,C, and D.[14] Notice that we can therefore make use of the indicators to enable us to infer the direction of causality between X and Y. *The third model is of particular interest in that we can infer a spurious relationship between X and Y even without any knowledge as to what Z is.* If both r_{ad} and r_{bc} are approximately zero, and if the remaining predicted relationships (e.g., r_{ab}, r_{bd}, and r_{cd} nonvanishing) are not too weak, we may have reasonably strong evidence of spuriousness. As usual, however, we must assume that the models are correct in other respects. For example there can be no direct links among the indicator variables, nor in the third model can A or C be associated with Z.

As we have emphasized throughout the chapter, *when dealing with unmeasured variables it will usually be advisable to make use*

14. In addition, all models make the predictions $r_{ac}=0$, $r_{ab}\neq0$, $r_{bd}\neq0$, and $r_{cd}\neq0$.

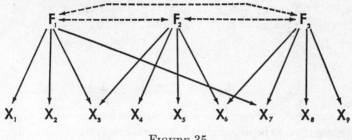

FIGURE 35

*of more than one indicator for each underlying variable in order
to obtain a degree of insurance against confounding influences.*
For instance, if we had a number of distinct indicators in the
positions of *A,B,C,* and *D* in Figures 32-34, then if we obtained
approximately the same results with each combination of indicators we might have additional faith in the conclusions
reached.

A Note on Factor Analysis. When used as a causal model,
factor analysis represents a special case of the type of analysis
under discussion in the present section. The rationale underlying factor analysis involves certain specific types of causal
models, namely those in which it is assumed that there are no
direct causal links among the indicator variables and that these
measured variables are caused by the underlying variables, making the intercorrelations among the indicators completely
spurious. One type of commonly used causal model providing
the theoretical rationale for factor analysis can be diagrammed
as in Figure 35.

Each of the measured variables X_i is supposedly caused by
one or more of the underlying factors F_i but not by any of the
remaining measured variables. The factors themselves may
or may not be causally interrelated, as indicated by the dashed
arrows. Using linear simultaneous equations we would write
each X_i as a function of the underlying variables plus an additional term e_i representing the effects of any variables that affect
X_i uniquely. Thus we will have a set of equations of the form

$$X_1 = a_1 + b_{11}F_1 + b_{12}F_2 + \ldots + b_{1k}F_k + e_1$$
$$X_2 = a_2 + b_{21}F_1 + b_{22}F_2 + \ldots + b_{2k}F_k + e_2$$

.

.

.

$$X_m = a_m + b_{m1}F_1 + b_{m2}F_2 + \ldots + b_{mk}F_k + e_m.$$

where the F_i represent the k unmeasured factors, where the e_i are assumed to be uncorrelated, and where certain of the b_{ij} may be zero. As is well known, there are an indefinitely large number of sets of factors that may satisfy these equations.

There is no need to go into further detail concerning factor analysis, since the procedures have been well described in the literature. But we should note the basic similarity to the rationale behind Simon's method. We are dealing, however, with a very restricted set of equations in that the *measured variables do not depend causally upon each other.* Any empirical intercorrelations among the X_i are presumed to be caused only by the underlying factors. The computing routines used to determine the various factors depend upon the idea that as each successive factor is "extracted," the average magnitudes of the intercorrelations among the X_i should be successively reduced. Finally, when all k factors have been extracted, the residual (partial) correlations should be zero or so near zero that their magnitudes can be attributed to sampling error.

But what if some of the measured variables were also caused by certain of the remaining measured variables? In some cases, then, there would be significant intercorrelations remaining after all k factors had been extracted. Unless we had specifically indicated which pairs of measured variables were directly linked causally, i.e., unless we had inserted additional terms involving these particular X_i into the appropriate equations, we might easily be misled into obtaining the "wrong" factors or into giving a poor interpretation for the factors we have extracted.

We should thus be explicitly aware of the fact that factor analysis techniques and the interpretations given to the factors extracted ordi-

narily presuppose certain limited kinds of causal models. In many empirical examples these causal assumptions would seem to be appropriate. Whenever the underlying factors are presumed to be internal psychological states and the measured variables responses to paper-and-pencil tests, we might legitimately assume that each of the individual responses is caused by one or more internal factors, plus of course certain stimuli from the environment, and that no response is caused by another response. Even here, we recognize the possibility that a response to one item may suggest a given response to another item, independent of any personality traits that may exist. We therefore attempt to mix up the items, change the wording, or make the connections between items as subtle as possible.

Suppose, however, that our measured variables consist of demographic variables such as educational and income levels, percentage of the labor force in manufacturing, or crime rates of various sorts. We wish to extract a number of underlying factors that can be used to characterize a city and that "account for" the various intercorrelations among the measured variables. Will the same sorts of causal models that provide the theoretical rationale for factor analysis still be appropriate? The problem becomes muddied. Perhaps it would be more reasonable to take educational levels as a direct cause of income levels than to account for their correlation in terms of some underlying factor that is even difficult to name. *The mere fact that factor analysis provides a technique for substituting a relatively small number of unmeasured variables for a larger number of measured variables does not mean that it should be used indiscriminately whenever the number of variables becomes too large for adequate conceptualization.* Unless the causal model is appropriate, the writer suspects that the analyst will have unusual difficulties in making sense out of, and giving names to, the various factors he has extracted.

CONCLUDING REMARKS

We have seen that predictions become less precise whenever we allow for the possibilities of measurement error and unmeasured variables, and, furthermore, it becomes necessary to introduce additional restrictive assumptions. With measurement errors and unmeasured variables the prediction equations involve inequalities rather than more exact relationships. We also have had to assume that unmeasured variables and unknown disturbance factors are linearly related to the other variables. This latter type of assumption might be plausible under certain circumstances. For example if $X \to Y \to Z$, with Y being unmeasured, then if we found a linear relationship between X and Z it would seem reasonable to conclude that Y is also linearly related to the two measured variables. But there will always be an upper limit to the number of such supposedly plausible assumptions one is willing to accept without demonstration.

It should be emphasized that although many of the assumptions imposed on a given model are in fact highly restrictive, most of these can in principle be modified. *Probably, however, it will be unrealistic to suppose that one can modify several such assumptions at once.* What if we wished to allow both for unmeasured variables and nonadditivity? Or we might attempt to use models involving two-way causation and also considerable measurement error. The complications introduced might very well be such that no really adequate empirical predictions could be made.

The apparent fact that research in the social sciences may often require the simultaneous lifting of several such restrictive assumptions points up the difficult path that lies ahead. But the situation is by no means hopeless. At the present time a high degree of precision cannot be expected, and we shall undoubtedly have to remain contented with exploratory uses of causal models rather than exact tests. We may therefore be willing to tolerate moderate outside disturbances or departures from linearity and still use the differential predictions from alternative causal models to give valuable insights.

As mentioned previously, we may have to pay a high premium for the inability to experiment, for the large number of variables with which we must deal, and for our crude measurement techniques. One reaction to these imperfections may very well be to give up the attempt to make use of deductive types of models that involve a large number of restrictive assumptions. Quite clearly, *a failure to state one's assumptions explicitly does not make them disappear in some magical way.* It *does, however, make it much more difficult to evaluate and reject a given theoretical system.* Theoretical inadequacies are harder to spot, and untestable theories remain to clutter up the literature. Such a state of affairs is hardly desirable.

VI

Summary and Conclusions

Since the previous chapters have covered a good deal of ground that may be unfamiliar to practicing social scientists, it might be well to summarize the principal arguments. For the convenience of the reader, this summary will be made on a chapter-by-chapter basis, with page references given in parentheses so that the more detailed discussion of each topic can be easily reviewed. This summary section will then be followed by a brief section dealing with implications and practical suggestions.

SUMMARY

Chapter I.

1. Owing to the inherent nature of the scientific method, there is a gap between the languages of theory and research. Causal inferences belong on the theoretical level, whereas actual research can only establish covariations and temporal sequences. (pp. 5-10).

2. As a result, we can never actually demonstrate causal laws empirically. This is true even where experimentation is possible. Causal laws are working assumptions of the scientist,

involving hypothetical statements of the *if-then* variety. (pp. 11-14).

3. Included among the *if*'s of causal assertions is the supposition that all relevant variables have been controlled or can safely be ignored. This kind of assumption can never be tested empirically. (pp. 13-14).

4. Causality is conceived in the present work as involving the notion of production, i.e., causes *produce* effects. This kind of notion is difficult to formalize, as in mathematical or logical systems. Nor is it subject to empirical verification. (pp. 9-10).

5. The notion of production introduces asymmetry into causal relationships. Temporal sequences are also asymmetrical but should not be confused with causal relationships. Nor should causality be confused with *prediction*, which refers to the state of the observer's knowledge. (p. 10).

6. In order to avoid empiricist objections to causal terminology, we prefer to think in terms of causal models of reality. These models can contain desired simplifications, such as the assumption that events can be replicated and the assumption that neglected factors operate in specified ways. (pp. 14-15).

7. Since these models do not refer to reality itself, and since a number of alternative models may yield the same predictions, we can never actually establish a given model. But we can proceed by eliminating or modifying inadequate models that give predictions inconsistent with the data. (pp. 20-21).

8. We choose to construct models that allow for disturbances created by variables left out of the theoretical system, but we must make certain assumptions about how these outside factors operate. Allowing for such disturbances is consistent with either a deterministic or an indeterministic philosophical position, given the limitations of scientific procedure. (pp. 15-18).

9. The notions of direct and indirect causes are defined as relative to the particular variables included in the system. If other variables were to be included, the causal model might have to be changed. There is thus no single "correct" model that can be demonstrated to be superior to all others. (pp. 18-20).

10. While the evaluation of causal models is made much simpler in experimental designs where randomization is possible, the same principles of inference apply to nonexperimental designs. In the latter, however, one's assumptions are likely to be much less plausible unless natural systems can be found that are practically isolated. (pp. 21 and 26).

11. Randomization helps us to make simplifying assumptions about a large class of "property" variables that can be made to operate independently of the causal variables under study. But other "forcing" variables cannot so readily be ruled out. Even in experimental designs, simplifying assumptions must always be made if causal models are to be evaluated. (pp. 24-26).

Chapter II.

1. The language of mathematics is a theoretical language, but it is not the same as causal language. We can therefore expect difficulties in translating back and forth between the two languages. In general, the mathematical language may permit too much flexibility in that mathematical paper-and-pencil operations may be easier to perform than physical operations and actual manipulations of factors. (pp. 27-30).

2. We choose to conceive of causal models in which variables are taken as continuous or at least capable of taking on a number of discrete values. Ideally, this presupposes an interval-scale level of measurement, though attributes may be taken as a special case. (pp. 32 and 34-35).

3. It is also possible to think in terms of attributes and necessary and sufficient conditions. However, it then becomes difficult to allow for disturbances and the use of arbitrary cutpoints. Hopefully, we can apply the same line of reasoning to all types of variables, whether these be attributes, ranked data involving ordinal scales, or legitimate interval scales. (pp. 30-34).

4. In mathematical equations, the distinction between dependent and independent variables is often arbitrary. There is thus a certain symmetry in the perfect mathematical function that does not correspond to causal asymmetry. The intro-

duction of error terms requires us to generalize the notion of a mathematical function to that of a regression equation, and another source of asymmetry is added in that the regression equation depends on one's choice of independent and dependent variables. (pp. 35-38).

5. In experiments there is apt to be much less confusion over which variable to take as independent than is the case in nonexperimental situations. Some implications of this fact are discussed in Chapter IV. (pp. 36-37).

6. The notion of prediction can easily be confused with that of a causal relationship. Prediction in the sense of estimation is a symmetrical matter: one can just as easily predict from the dependent to the independent variable. Practically, however, we often wish to predict to the dependent variable. (38-42).

7. The nonexperimental statistical literature is usually written as though interest is focused on a fixed population to which one wishes to generalize on the basis of sample data. The question of the causal mechanism producing this fixed set of scores is often ignored. (pp. 39-40).

8. The notion of "prediction" in the statistical literature often involves the notion that the goal is to estimate an individual's score on Y, given information about his scores on X_1, $X_2, \ldots, X_k$. To make such predictions we select the mean Y score for all individuals having the same combination of scores on the X_i. (p. 42).

9. This kind of prediction, however, does not enable one to assert how Y will *change* with given changes in the X_i. The mathematical kind of "changing" involves a paper-and-pencil substitution, rather than the kind of production change appropriate in causal terminology. The mathematical kind of change (substitution) involves a symmetrical relationship, giving the same results no matter which variable is taken as causally independent. Mathematical operations are again more flexible than physical operations. (pp. 41-43).

10. There are essentially two main uses for regression equations: as estimating equations and as causal equations. We are dealing only with the second usage. We should note that

variables that are most satisfactory for prediction purposes may be much less satisfactory if used in causal equations. (pp. 43-44).

11. In introducing error terms we must make certain assumptions about the variables that create these disturbances. The most restrictive assumptions would be that outside disturbing influences do not exist at all. Since we will seldom be in a position theoretically to specify upper limits to the amount of these disturbances, we shall find it necessary to make assumptions about *how* the outside influences are operating. (pp. 45-46).

12. We shall assume that error terms are uncorrelated with each other and with any of the independent variables in a given equation. This amounts to assuming that any outside variables causing the dependent variable Y are either small in magnitude and relatively numerous, or that one or two major causes of Y are unrelated to any of the independent variables included in the system. (pp. 46-48).

13. In nonexperimental studies involving nonisolated systems, this kind of assumption is likely to be unrealistic. This means that disturbing influences must be explicitly brought into the model. But at some point one must stop and make the simplifying assumption that variables left out do not produce confounding influences. Otherwise, causal inferences cannot be made. (p. 49).

14. In most realistic situations we must deal with more than one dependent variable. This forces us to consider a simultaneous set of equations rather than a single equation. These simultaneous equations often do not admit of simple solutions. (pp. 52-53).

15. In general, one cannot readily solve a set of equations in which each variable is taken to be dependent on *all* of the remainder. There will be too many unknowns for unique solutions, nor can simple assumptions about error terms be made. (pp. 53-54).

16. We therefore confine our attention to recursive systems of equations that can be handled by ordinary least squares. In

such equations we assume that if X_i causes X_j, then X_j cannot at the same time cause X_i. We can then write equations in which X_1 does not depend causally on any of the other variables; X_2 depends only on X_1, X_3 only on X_1 and X_2, and so forth. (pp. 54-55).

17. These recursive systems can then be linked readily with causal interpretations. They can also be used to handle reciprocal causation provided certain variables can be "lagged" at appropriate time intervals. (pp. 55-59).

18. In causal analyses our aim is to focus on causal laws as represented by regression equations and their coefficients. Major concern should therefore be focused on slopes rather than correlation coefficients, which merely measure amount of unexplained variation. An exception is where both coefficients can be expected to disappear, as in the testing of causal models. This point is amplified in Chapters III and IV. (pp. 50-52).

Chapter III.

1. Even restricting ourselves to recursive systems and one-way causal relationships, we cannot test the adequacy of a given causal model without making additional assumptions. These involve the presumed independence among error terms and the disappearance of certain of the b's. (pp. 63-64).

2. Setting a particular partial slope equal to zero gives the interpretation that there is no *direct* causal link between the two variables concerned, though there may be indirect linkages through other variables. The disappearance of a partial slope is equivalent to the disappearance of the comparable partial correlation, under ordinary least squares. (pp. 64-65).

3. For each slope assumed equal to zero, we obtain a condition that the data must satisfy in order for the model to be consistent with the data. Thus if three b's have been set equal to zero, there will be three fewer unknowns than equations, and we will have three conditions which the data must satisfy. These conditions can be thought of as prediction equations implied by the model in question. (pp. 64-65).

4. The prediction equations can be written in the form of some partial correlation set equal to zero. In general, this partial will involve the relationship between two variables not connected directly by a causal arrow, with controls for variables that are either causally prior to or intervening between these variables. (pp. 64-69).

5. In considering a predicted disappearance of a partial correlation between two variables not directly connected by a causal arrow, it is important that we do not attempt to control for variables that are causally dependent on both of these variables. Controlling for dependent variables would seem to have no counterpart in experimental situations. (pp. 66-67).

6. If a number of causal arrows have been eliminated, certain simplifications in the prediction equations may result. These will involve the disappearance of specific lower-order partials. In such instances, it may not be necessary to control for certain variables in order to have the partials disappear, though it will do no harm to retain these controls. (pp. 67-68).

7. It appears to be generally true that there will be no need to control for any variable that is causally linked to only one of the other variables in the system. This is in line with the position that any of the variables in the system can be assumed to be caused by outside variables, as long as these disturbances are themselves uncorrelated. (pp. 68-69).

8. In the simple causal chain $X \rightarrow Y \rightarrow Z \rightarrow W$, the partial between X and W will disappear if *either* of the intervening variables Y and Z are controlled. This result holds generally, at least for linear models. (p. 68).

9. In the case of more than four variables, it may be difficult to specify which, if any, lower-order partials should disappear in any given case. In analyzing these models it may prove helpful to begin by dealing only with the three or four causally prior variables, taking advantage of the fact that in recursive systems one need not consider any variables that do not appear in a given equation or in equations involving causally prior variables. (p. 70).

10. The method for making causal inferences may be applied

to models based on a priori reasoning, or it may be used in exploratory fashion to arrive at models which give closer and closer approximations to the data. (p. 71).

11. In cases where models are to be modified in ex-post-facto fashion, two practical rules are suggested: (a) start with variables assumed to be causally prior to the others and (b) make modifications where the largest discrepancies between predicted and actual results occur. These two rules of thumb may, of course, sometimes be incompatible. (p. 80).

12. The use of causal models of the type discussed in this work presupposes that certain assumptions can be met. Where this is not possible, certain complications arise that make it necessary to introduce some notes of caution. Additional complications are discussed in Chapter V. (pp. 83-94).

13. It may often in practice be difficult to distinguish spurious relationships from other models, as for example the case of a developmental sequence. This is particularly the case whenever measurement errors are considerable. Controls for so-called "background variables" are especially vulnerable to this kind of difficulty. (pp. 83-87).

14. Relationships among variables may be nonadditive, thus making for interaction effects. Certain types of nonadditive relationships (e.g., multiplicative ones) can easily be transformed into additive ones. (pp. 91-93).

15. The problem of multicollinearity arises whenever two or more "independent" variables are highly correlated. In such instances, sampling errors will be large and controls for other independent variables may be highly misleading. It will thus be difficult to assess the relative contributions of the various independent variables. (pp. 87-91).

Chapter IV.

1. In nonexperimental research the investigator may manipulate his variables, sometimes completely unconsciously. In such instances the amount of variation in both independent and dependent variables may be affected. (pp. 95-96).

2. If these manipulations involve the independent rather than the dependent variable, then under a number of circumstances slopes will remain approximately invariant, whereas correlation coefficients may change. This is owing to the fact that correlation coefficients merely measure the proportion of unexplained variation, which is a function of the degree to which outside variables vary as compared with variation in the independent variable. (pp. 101-1).

3. The implication of this fact is that in instances where partial correlations and slopes cannot be expected to disappear, the focus of attention should be primarily on slopes and on the regression equation itself. The current focus on correlation coefficients may be owing to the fact that in most instances there is considerable unexplained variation. (pp. 100-1 and 113).

4. Whenever we shift units of analysis (e.g., from persons to groups, from counties to states) this kind of problem arises. In shifting to larger units we affect the amount of variation in all variables, including unknown factors affecting the dependent variable. In general, the larger the units, the less the variation. (pp. 97-99).

5. The degree to which the variation in each variable is reduced by using larger units is a function, however, of *how* the smaller units are put together. If put together randomly there should be no systematic effect on either the correlation or regression coefficients. (pp. 101-5).

6. It is possible to put together the smaller units in such a way as to maximize the variation in either the independent or dependent variable. In the former case, we can substantially increase the correlation because of the fact that variation in disturbing influences will be considerably reduced. The slope, however, will not be affected. (pp. 105-7).

7. But if we put units together so as to maximize the variation in the dependent variable, then we may hopelessly confound the effects of the independent variable with those of outside influences. (pp. 107-9).

8. In real life, units are apt to be combined nonrandomly (e.g., when counties are combined into states). In the case of

geographical units, contiguity is often the major criterion. But such combinations may approximate to some degree the situations in which units have been put together so as to maximize variation in either the independent or dependent variables. If so, the slopes and correlation coefficients will be affected accordingly. (pp. 111-12).

9. Unfortunately, we often cannot assess the effects of such grouping operations, nor do we know which variable is to be taken as dependent. If the grouping procedure happens to involve a manipulation of the dependent variable, rather than the independent variable, then this would seem to have no simple counterpart in experimental situations and interpretations must be made with extreme caution. (pp. 109-10).

10. The same sorts of problems arise whenever we are comparing two sets of data involving differing amounts of variation in the independent variable, relative to that in other causes of the dependent variable. Since the latter variables are usually unknown, it will be much more appropriate to compare slopes than correlation coefficients. (pp. 114-19).

11. A special difficulty is encountered in using categorized data, particularly dichotomies. One then loses information as to amount of variation, and slope analogues (e.g., differences of proportions) no longer behave properly. This is a distinct disadvantage of 2×2 tables and categorized variables in general. (pp. 119-24).

12. Comparisons of change data with data based on a single point in time involve the same difficulty, and again it makes more sense to compare slopes than correlation coefficients. (pp. 124-26).

Chapter V.

1. Variables that have not been measured cannot always be ignored, because they may be responsible for confounding effects and measurement errors. Unmeasured variables may be of theoretical interest in their own right, with measured variables being taken as mere indicators of no inherent theoretical interest. (pp. 127-28 and 162-63).

2. Complications owing to unmeasured variables may be extremely difficult to handle, but insights into certain simple situations can be obtained by developing causal models that include unmeasured variables. In some instances empirical predictions can be made by bypassing these variables. (p. 128).

3. No single method can be counted on for reducing or eliminating the effects of confounding influences. These can sometimes be rigidly controlled. Randomization may also take out the effects of some such factors, as can the use of contrasting designs. (pp. 129-31).

4. A method for reducing the variation in confounding influences is proposed. This procedure depends on our finding variables W_i, which are causes of the independent variable under study but which are only weakly related to the disturbing influences. If we then group cases so as to maximize the variation in the W_i, we will reduce the variation in the disturbing influences to a greater degree than we will reduce the variation in the independent variable. We may then get a better estimate of the regression coefficient. (pp. 132-42).

5. Since it will seldom be possible to know how the confounding influences are operating, it is recommended that the investigator group by a number of distinct causes of the independent variable, noting whether or not they give the same results. (p. 143).

6. Measurement errors generally attenuate both correlation and regression coefficients. Random measurement errors in the dependent variable, however, do not affect the expected value of the slope. (pp. 144 and 147).

7. In tests for spuriousness or in situations where there is an intervening variable (e.g., $X \leftarrow W \rightarrow Y$ and $X \rightarrow W \rightarrow Y$), if there is no measurement error in the "middle variable" (e.g., W), then correct causal inferences can be made. However, random measurement errors in the middle variable will lead to a nonvanishing partial in these instances. (pp. 147-49).

8. Investigators should therefore be careful to retain as much

accuracy as possible in their control variables. Controls for "background variables" are especially likely to involve large measurement errors and faulty inferences. (pp. 149-50).

9. The use of categorized data, particularly dichotomies, often introduces additional measurement error. This is especially the case when one wishes to use simultaneous controls using contingency methods. The dichotomization of control variables is shown to give less satisfactory results (with artificial data) than when more categories are used or when ordinal techniques are used. (pp. 151-55).

10. Grouping techniques can be used to reduce the effects of random measurement errors and also systematic errors that are not related to the independent variable. These techniques again depend on our finding variables that are causes of the independent variable but that are not related to the disturbing influences causing measurement error. (pp. 158-62).

11. If the unmeasured variables are of special interest, and if indicators can be unambiguously linked to these variables, then predictions can sometimes be derived even where certain correlations will be unknown. Generally, however, these predictions will not be very precise nor will they be as numerous as would be the case if all variables were measured. (pp. 162-66).

12. If indicators can be found which are properly related to unmeasured variables, it may be possible to infer direction of causality among the latter variables. (p. 166).

13. Factor analysis can be considered a special case of this type of analysis. But we must assume a model in which the only causes of the measured indicators are the unmeasured variables. Factor analysis may therefore not be appropriate for census data or other types of analyses in which some of the measured variables are caused by other measured variables. (pp. 167-69).

14. In general, the use of unmeasured variables in a causal model will add further untestable assumptions that make inferences more difficult. We should therefore attempt to keep the number of such variables to a minimum. Otherwise, we

will probably develop theories that are "top-heavy" in the sense
that they are overly complex while at the same time yielding
very few empirically verifiable predictions.

CONCLUDING REMARKS

It seems safe to conclude that the problem of making causal
inferences on the basis of nonexperimental data is by no stretch
of the imagination a simple one. A number of simplifying
assumptions must be made, perhaps so many that the goal would
seem almost impossible to achieve. The temptation may very
well be to give up the entire venture. But, as we have suggested
at a number of points, there may not be any satisfactory alternatives. Most likely, social scientists will continue to make
causal inferences, either with or without an explicit awareness of
these problems.

Perhaps it will turn out that many of these difficulties are
inherently insurmountable, given the limitations of our data.
But it is as yet too early to tell. If social science findings and
theories become cumulative in nature, and if measurement procedures continually improve, then the situation is by no means
hopeless. In fact, during the exploratory phases of any given
discipline where one is merely searching for variables and attempting to find better measures of these variables, many of the
problems and issues discussed in the present work will come up
only tangentially. As emphasized previously, however, we believe that sooner or later they must be faced in all of the nonexperimental social sciences.

What is obviously needed at this stage is considerably more
methodological research into the logic of causal inferences and
into the nature of the methods that can be used to deal with
specific types of complicating issues such as the existence of
measurement error, multicollinearity, nonadditivity, and confounding influences. Fortunately for sociologists, psychologists, and anthropologists a good deal of such research is presently being carried out by econometricians. Each discipline, however, will have to deal with its own unique problems. There is
little room for pessimism, it seems, until basic research has been

systematically carried out. At this point we have hardly scratched the surface.

The practicing social scientist working on substantive problems must, however, be given advice as to how to proceed under these limitations. In brief, we would suggest flexibility as the guiding theme. In our haste to become "scientific" we have perhaps overrigidly followed the few rules of inference which have been rigorously set forth. Thus many social scientists insist on proper sampling methods, significance tests that do not require normality assumptions, and statistical measures that do not violate the limitations of measurement procedures. This is all to the good, and we would certainly not suggest that these practices be abandoned. But there is a vast territory where explicit rules do not exist and where speculation has been allowed to roam freely. It is not entirely inconceivable that as rules are developed covering this latter region these rules may be found to imply different decisions from those suggested by present knowledge.

We may illustrate by returning to the question of measurement. Social scientists are becoming increasingly aware of the fact that product-moment correlations and regression equations require the assumption that an interval-scale level of measurement has been attained. Lacking this level of measurement, the "cautious" procedure would seem to be to drop back to the use of ordinal and nominal scales. The investigator is then not open to the criticism of the statistician. But in so doing, he may introduce further measurement error. As we have seen, the practice of using dichotomized variables not only adds to measurement error but it also may obscure range of variation and invalidate the use of slopes for comparative purposes. In a sense, then, we may lose information or introduce distortions both ways. The major question, which cannot be answered definitively at present, is the relative seriousness of the distortions in each case.

When we urge flexibility we mean that, under present circumstances, it would be extremely helpful if social scientists would develop the habit of contrasting the results of several *different* procedures. For example, data might be analyzed both by using ordinal or contingency techniques *and* by assuming interval scales. If conclusions or results differed, one might gain valuable insights as to why specific differences have occurred. Perhaps dichotomization of the control variable has introduced too much error. Perhaps there is nonadditivity or multidimensionality. Similarly, alternative types of controlling techniques might be used in the same research. As we have suggested previously at several points, multiple indicators may provide both additional insights and checks on the adequacy of one's inferences. Where possible, a shift in units of analysis (e.g., from counties to states) may also shed new light on the problem at hand.

Present practices and publication policies are undoubtedly unfavorable to such a strategy. Especially in reports to be read by laymen it might prove embarrassing if two different methods gave dissimilar results. Many readers would not appreciate the subtleties involved, and any stereotypes they might have concerning the imperfections of social science might be reinforced. A prospective author who attempts to make use of regression techniques where measurement has been too crude would almost certainly find his paper rejected by respectable journals. Nor does journal space often permit an author the luxury of reporting the similarities and differences between several different modes of analysis. In addition, there are undoubtedly pressures on the individual investigator to report only his "best" results in instances where different techniques have not given the same results.

While such practices are perfectly understandable, they seem regrettable from the standpoint of obtaining useful data for methodological studies. In effect, we may be throwing away valuable information that may be helpful in assessing empirically the pro's and con's of alternative approaches. It is for this reason that increased flexibility seems highly necessary. This is not to say that present rules should be disregarded and that speculation should replace empirically-minded interpretations.

But it may be premature to pretend to a degree of rigor that we have hardly attained.

We can suggest a series of practical steps that might be carried out in causal analyses. Needless to say, all steps may not be easy to accomplish, nor do we wish to imply that steps should be taken in exactly the same order as given below.

1. Provided one has obtained a reasonable unidimensional scale and at least a moderately large sample (e.g., 150 to 200 cases), treat the data as though an interval scale had been attained and obtain correlation and regression coefficients. Also carry out the analysis, however, in terms of more "conservative" practices and compare results of the two methods.

2. Develop a series of alternative models, according to the best available theoretical knowledge. Run preliminary tests of the adequacy of each model, and introduce additional models in ex-post-facto fashion as was done in the case of the census-data discrimination models discussed in Chapter III. These models will constitute a reasonable number of initial models from which a smaller subset will ultimately be retained.[1]

3. Check for nonlinearity and nonadditivity in the relationships. If either occurs, try to account for its existence by examining the nature of the measurement process or by assuming some relatively simple alternatives (e.g., multiplicative relationships). Where possible, transform these relationships into linear additive ones and proceed. Where interaction seems unpatterned, look for the disturbing effects of outside variables. If interactions are large and unpatterned, the analysis may have to be stopped at this point. In some instances it may be possible to find subsamples in which no interaction occurs or for which different causal models are appropriate.

1. For the convenience of the reader, I have worked out a table showing the predictions for forty-one four-variable causal models which cover all of the nontrivial possible models involving one-way causation. See H. M. Blalock, "Four-Variable Causal Models and Partial Correlations," *American Journal of Sociology*, LXVIII (September, 1962), 182-94. Unfortunately, the order of presentation of models in the table appearing in this paper was interchanged by typographical error. The table appears in more usable form in the *American Journal of Sociology*, LXVIII (January, 1963), 510-12.

4. Search for possible confounding influences that have not been brought into the model but that can plausibly be expected to operate. Develop models that include these confounding influences as unmeasured variables and examine their implications for the data. Where possible, try to find indicators of these confounding influences. Add the indicators to the model by assuming the indicator to be caused by (or to be a cause of) the confounding influence plus factors contributing random measurement error in the indicator. Note the implications and see if the data conform to expectations. If so, this would suggest that future research should involve more direct attempts to measure the confounding influence that has been postulated.

5. Examine the implications of the models in question when one allows for random measurement errors. If there are any obvious sources of nonrandom errors, construct models and examine their implications. Where errors may be produced by the fact that one has dropped back to lower levels of measurement (e.g., ordinal scales or dichotomies), compare results with those obtained using these lower levels of measurement.

6. Where possible, try to take out confounding influences and measurement errors by procedures similar to those suggested in Chapter V. Results of these operations will be highly tentative until knowledge can be built up cumulatively.

7. Where shifts in units of analysis or changes in design are possible, it will be helpful to compare results. For example, one may group geographical units by proximity and note what happens to b_{yx} and b_{xy}. Then it may be possible to account for any changes, as in the case of the relationship between per cent nonwhite and income differentials discussed in Chapter IV.

8. Be alerted to the possibility that independent variables may be highly correlated, in which case large sampling errors may prohibit one from assessing the relative influence of each variable.

9. Report the results of these exploratory investigations in the literature, even where shortcomings are obvious. This should make cumulative efforts more likely, and it will also provide data for further methodological work.

APPENDIX

APPENDIX

Some Related Approaches

There are at least several lines of attack on the problem of causal inferences which are distinctly related to the materials presented in the main body of this book but which have not been integrated with our own discussion. We shall only very briefly indicate the nature of two approaches that seem highly promising, while giving a short bibliography of items that the reader may wish to consult as initial sources leading to more detailed study.

Work by Donald Campbell and his associates has focused on a number of alternative "quasi-experiments" that can be used when randomization has not been possible but where temporal sequences can be noted or inferred. One approach discussed by Campbell involves "cross-lagging" procedures in which the direction of causality is inferred by examining the relative magnitudes of the correlations between two variables at different points in time. The essential idea is that the correlation between the causal variable at $time_1$ and the dependent variable at $time_2$ should be greater than that between the causal variable at $time_2$ and the effect variable at $time_1$. The method of course requires certain simplifying assumptions about error terms and would seem most appropriate whenever the time-lag between cause and effect is sufficiently long that it is commensurate with the intervals between observations.

Campbell has also emphasized the necessity of taking fallible measurement into consideration in instances where imperfect controlling operations lead to the "overinterpretation" of one's data. Because of tendencies of imperfectly measured variables to regress toward the mean, one may get reductions in the apparent magnitude of the relationship between two variables when controls are introduced, but these may be primarily owing to the artifacts of measurement error rather than to the inferred relationships among variables. Survey analysis with multiple cross-classifications is particularly vulnerable to this kind of difficulty. Campbell's cautions regarding the implications of measurement error are similar to those given in Chapters III and V.

The work of Sewall Wright and other biometricians on "path coefficients" also seems to be closely related in many respects to the approach we have been using. Path coefficients, which combine features of both the correlation and regression coefficients, are used to enable one to assess the relative contribution of a given factor to the correlation between two other variables. A rationale for partitioning an original correlation into component parts is developed which makes use of causal diagrams similar to the ones we have presented. In some respects the assumptions of the two approaches are similar, particularly with respect to the behavior of error terms and the nonexistence of measurement errors in the independent variables.

The method of path coefficients appears to be primarily useful in situations where practically all of the variation in a given dependent variable can be associated with the other variables explicitly included in the system. It also seems to be most appropriate where theory has been well developed and where it is merely necessary to estimate the magnitudes of empirical constants. But the methods and ideas involved might readily be modified or extended so as to be highly useful in the less precise nonexperimental sciences.

Bibliographical items are listed below in alphabetical order since in all instances the titles are self-explanatory. In the case of path coefficient theory, the two items by C. C. Li are recommended as good starting points for the nonmathematical reader.

Campbell, D. T., "Quasi-Experimental Designs for Use in Natural Social Settings," in D. T. Campbell, *Experimenting, Validating, Knowing: Problems of Method in the Social Sciences* (New York: McGraw-Hill Book Company, in press).

Campbell, D. T., and K. N. Clayton, "Avoiding Regression Effects in Panel Studies of Communication Impact," *Studies in Public Communication*, No. 3 (Chicago: Department of Sociology, University of Chicago, 1961), pp. 99-118.

Campbell, D. T., and J. S. Stanley, "Experimental and Quasi-Experimental Designs for Research on Teaching," in N. L. Gage (ed.), *Handbook of Research on Teaching* (Chicago: Rand McNally & Company, 1963), pp. 171-246.

Li, C. C., "The Concept of Path Coefficient and Its Impact on Population Genetics," *Biometrics*, XII (June, 1956), 190-210.

Li, C. C., *Population Genetics* (Chicago: University of Chicago Press, 1955), Chapter 12.

Turner, M. E., and C. D. Stevens, "The Regression Analysis of Causal Paths," *Biometrics*, XV (June, 1959), 236-58.

Wright, S., "The Method of Path Coefficients," *Annals of Mathematical Statistics*, V (September, 1934), 161-215.

Wright, S., "Path Coefficients and Path Regressions: Alternative or Complementary Concepts?," *Biometrics*, XVI (June, 1960), 189-202.

Wright, S., "The Treatment of Reciprocal Interaction, With or Without Lag, in Path Analysis," *Biometrics*, XVI (September, 1960), 423-45.

INDEX

Index